104
Attributes & Actions
of
GOD

*Characteristics of God
in Psalms Bible Study,
Praise & Prayer Devotional*

EJ JANIK

Carpenter's Son Publishing

104 Attributes and Actions of God

©2018 by EJ Janik

Second Edition
First Edition ©2017

Published by Carpenter's Son Publishing, Franklin, Tennessee. Published in association with Larry Carpenter of Christian Book Services, LLC. www.christianbookservices.com

Edited by Bob Irvin

Cover and Interior Layout Design by Suzanne Lawing

Printed in the United States of America

978-1-946889-37-9

Sourcing, Methodology, and Project Background

I am a forensic accountant and CPA. By definition, this means I use my accounting training and knowledge, combined with investigative and fact-finding skills, in areas that include accounting, financial, construction claims, fraud, business disputes, auditing, and experience serving as an expert witness. My business is in Dallas, and I have more than thirty-five years of experience in the field.

What does this have to do with studying the characteristics of God in the Psalms? For myself, it had everything to do with the project before you. It is more than a project, however. It is a passion, a way to connect with God, a way to understand God's attributes and actions.

Some months ago, when I looked back at the seven years I put into this study, I realized I had used my areas of expertise to construct this work: fact-finding, analytical skills, the process of examination. I have discovered, researched, cross-referenced, studied, counted, and verified the characteristics of God.

What I discovered is that, in the Psalms, there are at least forty-four attributes and sixty actions of God, Lord, and the Lord God. This is based on more than twelve hundred Scriptures in this astounding collection, including the use of Hebrew words and various translations.

Allow me, however, a moment to take a step back. Growing up Catholic, I would hear about God in two main ways: in Mass and from the book of Psalms. In my twenties I read Psalms and Proverbs in my small Gideon Bible. Later, I joined my wife's Methodist Church and found myself teaching our Sunday school class, doing so for more than five years. That is when I started my deepest reading and study of the Bible; this included listening to numerous Chuck Swindoll lessons.

My faith journey expanded even more when we moved to Dallas and worshiped under great pastors and teachers at Northwest Bible Church, Bent Tree Bible, and now at Prestonwood Baptist Church. This included teaching roles in the preteen and teenage boy programs. Our Sunday school and Fellowship teachers also positively influenced me. Numerous Bible scholars from Dallas Theological Seminary also significantly impacted my life and study of the Bible.

This was my personal approach: for years, on a daily basis, I would read one chapter of Proverbs and five chapters in the Psalms. Soon my underlining and highlighting and the various notes in my Bible led to something revelatory: I saw the numerous characteristics of God. And for the last seven years, in my self-study, I compiled the attributes and actions of God that I observed. Then I researched those verses by studying the Hebrew and other translations. And this led to my categorization of these 104 attributes and actions of God. In Psalms:

- *God* is used 429 times

- *LORD* can be found 791 times

I did not otherwise include this information in this study guide and devotional, but one can see the voluminous number of times God's name is used in this one book of the Bible alone.

~~~

Below is my sourcing for this study, and a word about methodology.

1. **My original Bible source:** *Ps.* = Psalm NIV Life Application Bible, New International Version, 1991, Published by Tyndale House Publishers, Inc., Wheaton, Illinois; and Zondervan Publishing House, Grand Rapids, Michigan; or use of the NIV per BlueLetterBible.org[a].

2. **Strong's Exhaustive Concordance:** use of Strong's through BlueLetterBible.org[a]

3. **Hebrew:** References are obtained from the Wave Study Bible, BlueLetterBible.org,[a] or both.

4. **Other versions or translations:** obtained from Wave Study Bible[a], and sorted alphabetically:
   a. English Standard Version
   b. God's Word Translation
   c. King James
   d. New American Standard Bible
   e. New English Translation
   f. New International
   g. New International Reader's Version
   h. New King James Version

  i. New Living Translation

  j. The Message

5. **Word frequency in the Psalms:** This was developed through BlueLetterBible.org, and I have included examples of those relating to God and/or Lord.

6. **Attributes of God:** further developed from Moms In Touch International, August 2010.[b]

7. **Internet Research:** Often I would search for God's characteristics. For example: "*When* did God answer in the Bible?"

~~~

8. **Other books that describe the attributes of God that I have considered include**:

  A. *The Attributes of God*, Arthur W. Pink, paperback $10.99, 2006, ISBN: 978-0-8010-6772-3, 123 pages

   • God's attributes include: solitariness, decrees, knowledge, foreknowledge, supremacy, sovereignty, immutability, holiness, power, faithfulness, goodness, patience, grace, mercy, love, wrath, contemplation.

  B. *The Attributes of God,* A. W. Tozer, Volume 1, A Journey Into the Father's Heart with Study Guide, 2003, paperback, $15.99, ISBN: 978-1-60066-129-7, 306 pages

   • God's attributes include: infinitude, immensity, goodness, justice, mercy, grace, omnipresence, immanence, holiness, perfection.

  C. *The Attributes of God,* A. W. Tozer, Volume 2, Deeper Into the Father's Heart with Study Guide, 2003, paperback, $15.99, ISBN: 978-1-60066-138-9, 317 pages

   • God's attributes include: God's character, self-existence, transcendence, eternalness, omnipotence, immutability, omniscience, wisdom, sovereignty, faithfulness, love.

  D. *The Power of God's Names*, Tony Evans, 2014, paperback, $14.99, ISBN: 978-0-7369-3997-3

   • The fourteen names include: Creator; Relational God, God who rules, Provider, Warrior, Peace, Shepherd, Banner, Lord who sanctifies, Healer,

My Righteousness, Most High God, Lord God Almighty, God With Us.

Methodology: I researched various word alternatives including word endings of es, ed, and er; and present and past noun, adjective, and adverb tenses. Examples: save, saves, saved, savior.

~~~

I would like to provide a word of thanks. My deepest gratitude goes primarily to Tina Golden, along with Eric Matthaei and Leah Janik for their fact-finding, editing, refining, and reviewing. I am also very grateful for our small group that met bimonthly to study my first draft.

Most importantly, I thank God for my dear loving wife and prayer warrior of forty-three years. God truly orchestrated us to meet forty-seven years ago! Leah is a Proverbs 31 woman and my best friend on this earth. God has has blessed us with two sons, Grant and Tyler, who have honored us in so many ways.

(a) WaveStudyBible.com. I have not repeated the specific characteristic of God in each section.
(b) https://momsinprayer.org. Moms in Prayer International. The organization was formerly called Moms In Touch International.

Seeing God Through the Psalms

As I began an intense study of the Psalms, one of the first questions I began to ask myself was this: *what do we learn about God, and the nature of God Himself, from the Psalms?*

Through seven years of study, I have drawn these conclusions.

In the Psalms, there are **44 attributes and 60 actions of God** that we can clearly identify. I develop these in detail in the 104 study chapters in this book.

God's Attributes include:

Almighty	Gracious	Refuge
Anger	Great	Righteous
Awesome	Holy	Rock
Compassionate	Hope	Savior
Creator	Justice	Shepherd
Dwells	Kind	Sovereign
Enthroned	Knows	Splendor
Eternal (Forever)	Light/Lights	Strength
Faithful	Majestic	Strong
Father	Merciful	Stronghold
Feared	Mighty	Trustworthy
Flourisher	Miraculous	Warrior
Fortress	Peace Giver	Wonders
Glorious	Perfect/Perfector	Wonderful
Good	Present	

God's Actions include:

Answers	Comforts	Crushes
Avenges	Commands	Defends
Bears	Confronts	Delivers
Blesses	Contends	Despises
Cleanses	Counsels	Destroys

Disciplines	Instructs	Relieves
Enables	Judges	Remembers
Encourages	Knows	Rescues
Examines	Lifts	Restores
Forgives	Listens	Rewards
Forsakes	Looks	Saves
Gives	Loves	Shelters
Grants	Makes	Shields
Guards	Preserves	Silences
Guides	Promises	Speaks
Heals	Protects	Supports
Hears	Provides	Sustains
Helps	Punishes	Teaches
Hides	Rebukes	Upholds
Humbles	Redeems	Watches

God is active, connective, and interactive. For so many, God may be Creator, Father of Jesus, and Lord God of all. And yet, He is not one who trifles with our everyday lives. He is involved in His business, but He does not come down to ours *(or, mine)*. Simply put, God is way above my level.

But the Psalms tell us this is simply not true. Through this study, you will see that God is *involved*—active, desiring to connect with you, desiring to interact with you as you make day-to-day choices and decisions.

God reveals Himself in the Psalms. The entire Bible, of course, is revelatory about God. But in Psalms we see more of the nature, character, depths—*soul, will, and love*—of God. This study will be an aid to help you see who God truly is.

Jesus refers to the God of the Bible through the Psalms. Jesus quoted the book of Psalms more than any other book: anywhere from eleven to sixteen different times, according to varying accounts.[a] (Deuteronomy, Isaiah, and Exodus are the three books Jesus most quoted after Psalms, if you are curious.) Among them: quoting the twenty-second Psalm while dying on the cross (Psalm 22:1 in Matthew 27:46 and Mark 15:34); that He was hated without cause (Psalm 35:19 in John 15:25); and even His recalling the manna in the wilderness after feeding five thousand (Psalm 78:24 in John 6:31).

The Psalms will give you insights to understand many important *truths* about God. There is so much about God we will never know. But the Psalms provide us many truths. You will see these unveiled in the 104 chapters.

Can You Answer the Following?

Conclusions are one thing, perhaps an end of the matter, as far as our limited minds can take us. But we start with questions. These are among the most important questions I began to ask myself as I studied the Psalms.

1. **Who is God?** Who, really, is this Creator of the universe? What can we know about Him? With certainty? Does He care about man? Why does He trifle with man? What things are indelible in the character of God?

   God Is: Almighty, Awesome, Creator, Eternal, Glorious, Holy, Majestic, Mighty, Perfect, Righteous

2. **Do you know God?** This is a much different question from the first one. Do I know God? Do I know him as I might a friend? A good friend? A closest friend? Do we even have a relationship? Is it a strong one? Lasting one? How well do I know Him?

   God Is: Faithful, Great, Kindness, Wonderful
   God: Helps, Lifts, Perseveres, Protects, Provides, Supports

3. **Do you know what God is like?** This, too, is somewhat different. What is the personality of God? Think of the question: To what is He *like*, or to what (on earth, of human knowledge and experience) could we compare Him? Isaiah 55 makes it clear that God is very unlike us—His ways higher than our ways. But the very existence of Jesus—His incarnation—also makes it clear that there are human personalities and tendencies that could, at least in some measure, shed important light on the being of God.

   God is: Good, Merciful, Miraculous
   God: Redeems, Teaches

4. **Does God know my future?** This, of course, is one of man's chief questions of himself, his generation, his entire species. What lies ahead of us—both on this earth and after death? Can the God of the Psalms help us answer that question? Not as well as we would like in this life, but the answer is an unqualified yes.

   God: Guides, Helps, Instructs
   God is: Present

5. **Does God see and know everything we do?** God is commonly called omniscient and omnipresent. Is He? What do the Psalms tell us about His ability to perceive all things in

our lives?

God: *Answers, Commands, Judges, Knows, Makes, Refreshes, Remembers, Sustains, Watches,*

God is: *a Refuge*

6. **What are important truths about God?** In the first part of this section, I wrote that my study began to provide meaningful insights into truths about God. The Psalms provide a great many truths—and uncover many attributes of God otherwise unknown.

God: *Bears, Delivers, Grants, Hides, Humbles, Redeems, Restores*

God is: *to Be Feared, Compassionate, Exhibits the Supernatural, Justice, Peace Giver*

7. **What are those attributes unique only to God?** I wrote that God supernaturally exhibits or shares human attributes and tendencies, and so He does. But a number of characteristics of God are not displayed in any human. What are they? How can we know the similar attributes with man, and those which are not?

God is: *a Flourisher, a Fortress, Hope, Light, Perfect, Savior, Sovereign, Splendor*

God: *Forgives (He Blots Out), Forsakes, Saves*

8. **What is your mental impression of God?** Perhaps this would have been a better starting place, for we must begin at the beginning—with what we think of God, our image of God. Our starting place is just that—but we must be aware of it before we can begin to deconstruct false perceptions.

God is: *Enthroned, Full of Wonders, Glorious, Gracious, Strong, Trustworthy*

9. **Which of God's attributes and actions are humanlike and yet supernatural?** A question that is different from numbers 3 and 7 above in this way: what characteristics does God display that exists in human life, but which He delivers in ways that are supernatural (above what is possible in nature), above our ability to display them?

God: *Dwells, Heals, Hears, Humbles, Listens, Looks (Observes), Silences, Speaks*

10. **How dependable is God?** Isn't this question critical? If I am going to pursue God, will He hear me, answer me—dare we even say it?—reward me? Will He be there? We speak of loyalty and faithfulness in human relationships and endeavors; how faithful will God be to me?

God is: *Faithful, a Flourisher, Hope, Strength*

God: Blesses, Enables, Encourages, Promises

11. ***How involved is God in my life?*** I wrote of this in the first half of this section, but the question still exists: how involved? Can this be measured in any way? Can this be tangibly felt?

God: Cleanses, Comforts, Counsels, Encourages, Examines, Relieves, Rescues, Shields

12. ***What are the parent-like attributes of God?*** Say, those most like a nurturing mother? A father who provides courage deep in the soul of his child? A disciplining father? A father who shows boundless and unconditional love?

God: Counsels, Defends, Disciplines, Forgives, Gives, Guards, Loves, Punishes, Rewards, Shelters, Teaches

God is: Father

13. ***What are my favorite characteristics of God?*** If God has emotions and feelings like us, He has attributes and qualities that we might admire most in some of the people around us. In God, however, these would be perfected. What about God's character would you list as your favorite attributes, traits, or characteristics?

God is: a Rock, a Shepherd, a Stronghold, Wonderful

14. ***What are the corrective characteristics of God?*** If God is a Father, He will treat us as any loving Father would, including correcting, rebuking, disciplining (see Hebrews 12 for more).

God: Avenges, Confronts, Contends, Crushes, Despises, Destroys, Disciplines, Punishes

God is: Anger/Angry, a Warrior

15. ***Once I begin to know God, will He be my "Lord" and my "Lord God"?*** We'll unpack this important question through the devotionals in this book.

Conclusion

Through this study you will see how God answers and avenges, blesses and bears, comforts and confronts, delivers and destroys, and much, much more. It is only a starting place to say the eternal God—the God of the Psalms—is wonderfully awesome and multifaceted. This is like saying the heavens are high or the oceans are deep. When we say it, we are speaking only in generalities, and we lack a complete understanding of the depth of the truths before us.

You are about to see the attributes and actions of God categorized, detailed, even proven, in numerous ways. My hope is that this study will move you to new places in your own study, appreciation, knowledge, and awe of God.

EJ JANIK
Dallas, Texas
August 2018
EJ@JanikPC.com

(a) Among the sites discussing Jesus' mention of the Psalms:
http://blog.biblia.com/2014/04/which-old-testament-book-did-jesus-quote-most/.

Devotionals

Chapter	God's Attribute or Action	# of Verses
1	Almighty	12
2	Anger	17
3	Answers	15
4	Avenges	7
5	Awesome	10
6	Bears	1
7	Blesses	13
8	Cleanses	2
9	Comforts	5
10	Commands	18
11	Compassionate	12
12	Confronts	1
13	Contends	2
14	Counsels	2
15	Creator	5
16	Crushes	8
17	Defends	6
18	Delivers	30
19	Despises	3
20	Destroys	9
21	Disciplines	5
22	Dwells	7
23	Enables	1
24	Encourages	1
25	Enthroned	19
26	Eternal (Forever)	13
27	Examines	4
28	Faithful	20
29	Father	4

Chapter	God's Attribute or Action	# of Verses
30	Feared	4
31	Flourisher	2
32	Forgives/Blots Out	5
33	Forsakes	3
34	Fortress	13
35	Gives	26
36	Glorious	15
37	Good	18
38	Gracious	6
39	Grants	8
40	Great	19
41	Guards	4
42	Guides (Leads)	11
43	Heals	6
44	Hears	41
45	Helps	37
46	Hides	10
47	Holy	29
48	Hope	8
49	Humbles	3
50	Instructs	4
51	Judges	16
52	Justice	11
53	Kindness	3
54	Knows	10
55	Lifts	7
56	Light/Lights	16
57	Listens	8
58	Looks (Observes)	8
59	Loves	55
60	Majestic	5

Chapter	God's Attribute or Action	# of Verses
61	Makes	21
62	Merciful	20
63	Mighty	15
64	Miraculous	6
65	Peace Giver	3
66	Perfect/Perfector	4
67	Present	3
68	Preserves	15
69	Promises	12
70	Protects	16
71	Provides	13
72	Punishes	12
73	Rebukes	11
74	Redeems	10
75	Refreshes	2
76	Refuge	34
77	Relieves	3
78	Remembers	12
79	Rescues	26
80	Restores	13
81	Rewards	3
82	Righteous	27
83	Rock	18
84	Saves	25
85	Savior	25
86	Shelters	4
87	Shepherd	4
88	Shields	19
89	Silences	4
90	Sovereign	9
91	Speaks	4

Chapter	God's Attribute or Action	# of Verses
92	Splendor	8
93	Strength	20
94	Strong	7
95	Stronghold	10
96	Supports	3
97	Sustains	9
98	Teaches	22
99	Trustworthy	28
100	Upholds	9
101	Warrior	1
102	Watches	19
103	Wonderful	11
104	Wonders	11
	TOTAL PSALM SCRIPTURES	**1,223**

1

ALMIGHTY: God is most powerful, the God of angel armies, a majestic king, mighty one who rules over all. He is a sovereign God.

Ps. 24:10   "Who is he, this King of glory? The LORD <u>Almighty</u> . . . "

Ps. 46:7   "The LORD <u>Almighty</u> is with us; the God of Jacob is our fortress."

Ps. 68:14   "When the <u>Almighty</u> scattered the kings in the land, it was like snow fallen on Mount Zalmon."

Ps. 69:6   "LORD, the LORD <u>Almighty</u>, may those who hope in you not be disgraced because of me . . . "

Ps. 80:4   "How long, LORD God <u>Almighty</u>, will your anger smolder against the prayers of your people?"

Ps. 80:7   "Restore us, God <u>Almighty</u>; make your face shine on us, that we may be saved."

Ps. 80:14   "Return to us, God <u>Almighty</u>! Look down from heaven and see! Watch over this vine."

Ps. 80:19   "Restore us, LORD God <u>Almighty</u>; make your face shine on us, that we may be saved."

Ps. 84:8   "Hear my prayer, LORD God <u>Almighty</u>; listen to me, God of Jacob."

Ps. 84:12   "LORD <u>Almighty</u>, blessed is the one who trusts in you."

Ps. 89:8   "Who is like you, LORD God <u>Almighty</u>? You, LORD, are mighty, and your faithfulness surrounds you."

Ps. 91:1   "Whoever dwells in the shelter of the Most High will rest in the shadow of the <u>Almighty</u>."

a. Hebrew/Strong's/biblical use

- Yahweh, Jehovah, Adonai, who causes all things to be
- Master
- most powerful

- war, warfare, host
- royal
- God, angels, judges

b. Other versions/translations

- commander of armies
- God and Lord of Heaven's Armies
- God of Angel Armies
- God of Hosts
- heaven's armies
- hosts
- invincible warrior
- King
- King of glory
- Lord of armies
- majestic king
- Mighty King
- Mighty One
- most powerful
- Shaddai
- Sovereign God
- sovereign judge
- Sovereign Ruler over all
- who commands armies
- who rules over all
- who rules over us

c. Praise & Prayer Journal

1. How did God, The Almighty, display His power when tested against the gods of Baal by the prophet? (Among the answers: smoked sacrifice and water.)

2. What are biblical examples of this characteristic, attribute, or action of God, as One who displays unlimited power and authority? (Among the answers: Kept the Egyptians from His people while they were leaving Egypt; parting of the Red Sea; in other Scriptures: God is almighty, mighty, does whatever He pleases, nothing is impossible: Genesis 17:1; Job 6:4, 29:5; Ezekiel 1:24; Joel 1:15; Revelation 1:8, 4:8, 11:17, 15:3.)

2   **ANGER:** God's anger includes displeasure; wrath; and, at times, impatience—but He is also slow to anger.

Ps. 2:5   "He rebukes them in his <u>anger</u> and terrifies them in his wrath . . . "

Ps. 6:1   "Lord, do not rebuke me in your <u>anger</u> or discipline me in your wrath."

Ps. 7:6   "Arise, Lord, in your <u>anger</u>; rise up against the rage of my enemies. Awake, my God; decree justice."

Ps. 30:5   "For his <u>anger</u> lasts only a moment, but his favor lasts a lifetime; weeping may stay for the night, but rejoicing comes in the morning."

Ps. 60:1   "You have rejected us, God, and burst upon us; you have been <u>angry</u>—now restore us!"

Ps. 69:24 "Pour out your wrath on them; let your fierce <u>anger</u> overtake them."

Ps. 76:7   "It is you alone who are to be feared. Who can stand before you when you are <u>angry</u>?"

Ps. 78:38 "Time after time he restrained his <u>anger</u> and did not stir up his full wrath."

Ps. 78:49 "He unleashed against them his hot <u>anger</u>, his wrath, indignation, and hostility . . . "

Ps. 79:5   "How long, Lord? Will you be <u>angry</u> forever? How long will your jealousy burn like fire?"

Ps. 85:5   "Will you be <u>angry</u> with us forever? Will you prolong your <u>anger</u> through all generations?"

Ps. 86:15 "But you, Lord, are a compassionate and gracious God, slow to <u>anger</u>, abounding in love and faithfulness."

Ps. 90:11 "Who knows the power of your <u>anger</u>?"

Ps. 103:8 "The Lord is compassionate and gracious, slow to <u>anger</u>, abounding in love."

Ps. 106:29 " . . . they aroused the Lord's <u>anger</u> by their wicked deeds, and a plague broke out among them."

Ps. 106:40 "Therefore the Lord was <u>angry</u> with his people and abhorred his inheritance."

Ps. 145:8 "The Lord is gracious and compassionate, slow to <u>anger</u> and rich in love."

a. Hebrew/Strong's/biblical use

- anger, wrath
- heat
- burning (of rage, anger)

- hot
- displeasure
- fear, terror

- indignation
- enraged

b. Other versions/translations

- angry
- burning heat
- displeased
- displeasure

- fury
- impatient
- infuriate
- mad

- rage
- raging fury
- wildfire anger
- wrath

c. Praise & Prayer Journal

1. How did God show His anger against the Egyptians and others who attacked Israel?

2. What are other biblical examples of this characteristic, attribute, or action of God? (Among the answers: Against Solomon in his later years; In Nahum 1:2, the Lord is avenging and wrathful; In Romans 1:18, the wrath of God is revealed from Heaven against all ungodliness and unrighteousness of men; other Scriptures: Exodus 15:7, 32:10, 11, 20:4-6; Numbers 11:1, 2, 32:13; Deuteronomy 7:1-6, 9:8; 2 Kings 13:3, 17:18; Job 4:9; Isaiah 13:5, 51:20; Ezekiel 7:8.)

3. When has God been slow to anger in your life? (You can find this used three times in Psalms, noted in the list above.)

ANSWERS: God speaks, commands, listens, responds, fulfills, intervenes, resolves, reacts, hears, provides solutions, and "answers me."

Ps. 3:4   "I call out to the LORD, and he <u>answers</u> me from his holy mountain."

Ps. 4:1   "<u>Answer</u> me when I call to you, my righteous God. Give me relief from my distress; have mercy on me and hear my prayer."

Ps. 17:6   "I call on you, my God, for you will <u>answer</u> me; turn your ear to me and hear my prayer."

Ps. 20:1   "May the Lᴏʀᴅ <u>answer</u> you when you are in distress . . . "

Ps. 20:6   "He <u>answers</u> him from his heavenly sanctuary with the victorious power of his right hand."

Ps. 27:7   "Hear my voice when I call, Lᴏʀᴅ; be merciful to me and <u>answer</u> me."

Ps. 38:15   "Lᴏʀᴅ, I wait for you; you will <u>answer</u>, Lord my God."

Ps. 65:2   "You who <u>answer</u> prayer, to you all people will come."

Ps. 65:5   "You answer us with <u>awesome</u> and righteous deeds, God our Savior . . . "

Ps. 69:16   "<u>Answer</u> me, Lᴏʀᴅ, out of the goodness of your love; in your great mercy turn to me."

Ps. 69:17   "Do not hide your face from your servant; <u>answer</u> me quickly, for I am in trouble."

Ps. 86:1   "Hear me, Lᴏʀᴅ, and <u>answer</u> me, for I am poor and needy."

Ps. 86:7   "When I am in distress, I call to you, because you <u>answer</u> me."

Ps. 120:1   "I call on the Lᴏʀᴅ in my distress, and he <u>answers</u> me."

Ps. 143:7   "<u>Answer</u> me quickly, Lᴏʀᴅ; my spirit fails."

a. Hebrew/Strong's/biblical use

- said, speak, answer
- command, tell, call
- listen
- promised
- responds

b. Other versions/translations

- acknowledges
- commands
- fulfills
- gives feedback
- hears
- intervenes
- listens
- provides solutions
- reacts
- replies
- resolves
- responds
- satisfies
- speaks

c. Praise & Prayer Journal

1. How many times has God answered you in your prayers? (You can find this use ten times in Psalms.)

2. What are biblical examples of this characteristic, attribute, or action of God? (Answers could include: Rachel, at one time childless; Hannah praying for a child, Samuel; Daniel fasted and prayed and Gabriel arrived and provided an answer; answering the prayers of Zechariah and Elizabeth, parents of John the Baptist; other Scriptures: Isaiah 65:24; Jeremiah 29:12; Matthew 7:7; John 14:13, 14, 16:24; James 1:5.)

3. Do you call—and wait—on God for His answers?

4

AVENGES: God redeems, displays His vengeance, avenges, and punishes, including revenging.

Ps. 3:7	"Arise, Lord! Deliver me, my God! <u>Strike</u> all my enemies on the jaw . . . "
Ps. 9:12	"For he who <u>avenges</u> blood remembers . . . "
Ps. 18:47	"He is the God who <u>avenges</u> me . . . "
Ps. 53:5	"God <u>scattered</u> the bones of those who attacked you; you put them to shame, for God despised them.
Ps. 64:7	"But God will <u>shoot</u> them with his arrows; they will suddenly be <u>struck down</u>."
Ps. 79:10	"Before our eyes, make known among the nations that you <u>avenge</u> the outpoured blood of your servants."
Ps. 94:1	"The Lord is a God who <u>avenges</u>. O God who <u>avenges</u>, shine forth."

a. Hebrew/Strong's/biblical use

- redeem
- rise, arise, stand
- wound / slaughter
- vengeance

b. Other versions/translations

- avenging
- makes inquisition for
- punish
- punishment

- revenging
- smitten, slapped, struck
- tracks down, pays back

c. Praise & Prayer Journal

1. When did God avenge for His people in the Bible? (Answers could include: while departing for Egypt, during the plagues in Egypt.)

2. What are other biblical examples of God avenging or punishing, like the enemies of Israel? (Answers could include: while departing Egypt, Sodom and Gomorrah; the tumbling walls of Jericho; the Lord avenges the Philistines by Samson [Judges 16]; David's victory over Goliath; other Scriptures: Leviticus 19:18; Proverbs 20:22, 24:29; Nahum 1:2; 1 Thessalonians 4:6; Hebrews 10:30.)

3. When have you seen God avenge in a situation?

5 **AWESOME**: God is to be feared, revered, honored, respected, and is wonderful, mighty, stunning; He is known by his inspiring, awesome deeds.

Ps. 45:4   "In your majesty ride forth victoriously in the cause of truth, humility and justice; let your right hand achieve <u>awesome</u> deeds."

Ps. 47:2   "For the LORD Most High is <u>awesome</u>, the great King over all the earth."

Ps. 65:5   "You answer us with <u>awesome</u> and righteous deeds, God our Savior, the hope of all the ends of the earth and of the farthest seas."

Ps. 66:3   "How <u>awesome</u> are your deeds! So great is your power that your enemies cringe before you.

Ps. 66:5   "Come and see what God has done, his <u>awesome</u> deeds for mankind!"

Ps. 68:35   "You, God, are <u>awesome</u> in your sanctuary . . . "

Ps. 89:7   "He is more <u>awesome</u> than all who surround him."

Ps. 106:22   " . . . miracles in the land of Ham and <u>awesome</u> deeds by the Red Sea."

Ps. 111:9   "He provided redemption for his people; he ordained his covenant forever—holy and <u>awesome</u> is his name."

Ps 145:6   "They tell of the power of your <u>awesome</u> works—and I will proclaim your great deeds."

a. Hebrew/Strong's/biblical use

- marvelous
- to fear

- to honor, respect
- to revere, be afraid

b. Other versions/translations

- awe-inspiring
- highly / greatly feared
- highly respected
- honored, honor

- inspiring
- mighty
- revere
- reverend

- stunning
- terrifying
- to be feared
- wonderful

c. Praise & Prayer Journal

1. What are some of God's awesome deeds? (Answers could include: protecting Israel from the Egyptians, parting of the Red Sea and the Jordan River, providing food for forty years in the desert, the tumbling walls at Jericho.)

2. What are other biblical examples of this characteristic, attribute, or action of God? (Possible answers: The Lord will fight for you while you keep silent [Exodus 14:14]; He has awesome power [Deuteronomy 4:34, 7:19, 9:29]; His awesome signs and wonders [Deuteronomy 6:22]; His awesome acts [2 Samuel 7:23]; "Yahweh is with me as an awesome, mighty one" [Jeremiah 20]; God gave His only begotten son [John 3:16].)

3. How has God been awesome in your life, and in the life of your family and friends?

6 **BEARS**: God loads us with benefits, carries us in His arms, and carries our burdens and heavy loads.

Ps. 68:19   "Praise be to the LORD, to God our Savior, who daily <u>bears</u> our burdens."

a. Hebrew/Strong's/biblical use

- be borne, load, put
- to load, impose a burden

b. Other versions/translations

- bears up
- carries our burdens for us
- carries our heavy loads
- carries us along
- carries us in His arms
- loads us with benefits

c. Praise & Prayer Journal

1. When has God borne your burden or your family's burden?

2. What are biblical examples of this characteristic, attribute, or action of God? (Answers could include: Abraham, Isaac, Jacob, and Joseph; God pledges to carry our burdens [Psalms 55:22]; "The Lord your God will hold your right hand" [Isaiah 41:13]; God will carry His flock in His bosom [Isaiah 46:11].)

3. What should you give to God to bear? Name an ongoing burden or heavy load.

 7 **BLESSES**: God rewards, does what is right, favors, empowers, supplies, and grants.

Ps. 5:12   "Surely, LORD, you <u>bless</u> the righteous; you surround them with your favor as with a shield."

Ps. 28:9	"Save your people and <u>bless</u> your inheritance; be their shepherd and carry them forever."
Ps. 29:11	"The LORD gives strength to his people; the LORD <u>blesses</u> his people with peace."
Ps. 37:22	"Those the Lord <u>blesses</u> will inherit the land, but those he curses will be destroyed."
Ps. 67:1	"May God be gracious to us and <u>bless</u> us and make his face shine on us."
Ps. 67:6	"The land yields its harvest; God, our God, <u>blesses</u> us."
Ps. 67:7	"May God <u>bless</u> us still, so that all the ends of the earth will fear him."
Ps. 115:12	"The LORD remembers us and will <u>bless</u> us: He will <u>bless</u> his people Israel."
Ps. 115:13	"He will <u>bless</u> the house of Aaron, he will <u>bless</u> those who fear the LORD— small and great alike."
Ps. 118:26	"<u>Blessed</u> is he who comes in the name of the LORD. From the house of the LORD we bless you."
Ps. 132:15	"I will <u>bless</u> her with abundant provisions; her poor I will satisfy with food."
Ps. 134:3	"May the LORD bless you from Zion, he who is the Maker of heaven and earth."
Ps. 147:13	"He strengthens the bars of your gates and blesses your people within you."

a. Hebrew/Strong's/biblical use

- blessed
- happy

b. Other versions/translations

- do what is right
- empower
- favored
- grants
- reward
- supply
- You mark us with blessing

c. Praise & Prayer Journal

1. How did God bless Israel and His people in the Old Testament?

2. What are other biblical examples of this characteristic, attribute, or action of God? (Among the answers: Abraham [Genesis 12:1-3, 22:17]; Isaac [Genesis 26:24]; Jacob [Genesis 27:27-29, 28:12-15; Jacob at Bethel, Genesis 35]; God's hand on Ezra and Nehemiah [Ezra 7:6, 7:10, 8:18, 8:22, 8:31; Nehemiah 2:8, 2:18]; no good thing does He withhold from those who walk uprightly [Psalm 84:11].)

3. How has God blessed you, your family, your work and business, our country?

8 CLEANSES: God purifies, purges, makes clean and pure, washes, scrubs away.

Ps. 51:2   "Wash away all my iniquity and <u>cleanse</u> me from my sin."

Ps. 51:7   "<u>Cleanse</u> me with hyssop, and I will be clean . . . "

a. Hebrew/Strong's/biblical use

- clean, purify, purge
- to be pure
- to make white, clean

b. Other versions/translations

- purge
- purify
- to make clean
- to make pure
- wash, scrub away

c. Praise & Prayer Journal

1. Who in the Bible was cleansed by God? (David, following his sins with Bathsheba, is a preeminent example.)

2. What are other biblical examples of this characteristic, attribute, or action of God? (Answers could include: The Day of Atonement shall be "made for you to cleanse you and you will be clean from your sins before the Lord" [Leviticus 16:30]; when the Lord washed away filth [Isaiah 4:4]; "I will cleanse them from all of their iniquity" [Jeremiah 33:8]; Thus says the Lord God "on the day that I cleanse you from all your iniquities" [Ezekiel 36:33]; God's fountain cleanses us from sin and impurity [Zechariah 13:1].)

3. Should we ask God to cleanse us of past sins and shortcomings? How should you approach God in doing so?

9 **COMFORTS**: God strengthens, reassures, give courage, makes us feel secure, consoles, and comforts.

Ps. 23:4   "I will fear no evil, for you are with me; your rod and your staff, they <u>comfort</u> me."

Ps. 71:21   "You will increase my honor and <u>comfort</u> me once more."

Ps. 86:17   " . . . for you, LORD, have helped me and <u>comforted</u> me."

Ps. 94:19   "When anxiety was great within me, your <u>consolation</u> brought joy to my soul."

Ps. 119:52   "I remember, LORD, your ancient laws, and I find <u>comfort</u> in them."

a. Hebrew/Strong's/biblical use

- comfort, consolation
- compassion, solace
- to be sorry, repent, be comforted
- to strengthen

b. Other versions/translations

- assuring words
- be tender to me
- console, consolation
- feel secure
- give courage
- on the right track
- reassure
- renewed hope
- to strengthen

c. Praise & Prayer Journal

1. Was Job eventually comforted by God? (Possible answers: Yes, both after Satan's attack and after he received criticism from his friends.)

2. What are biblical examples of this characteristic, attribute, or action of God? (Answers could include: Sarah's servant Hagar, Moses, Joshua, Rahab, Mary, Peter; other Scriptures: The Lord himself "goes before you and will be with you" [Deuteronomy 31:8, 9]; "'Comfort my people,' says your God" [Isaiah 40:1]; God is God of all comfort: "I even I am He who comforts you" (Isaiah 51:12); as a mother comforts so will God comfort you [Isaiah 66:13].)

3. When has God comforted you and your family? (You can find the phrase "comforts me" three times in the Psalms; these are noted at the top of this chapter.)

10 COMMANDS: God counsels, orders, tells, directs, promises.

Ps. 19:8   "The commands of the Lord are radiant, giving light to the eyes."

Ps. 33:9   "For he spoke, and it came to be; he commanded, and it stood firm."

Ps. 78:5   "He decreed statutes for Jacob . . . which he commanded our ancestors to teach their children."

Ps. 78:23   "Yet he gave a command to the skies above and opened the doors of the heavens."

Ps. 91:11   "For he will command his angels concerning you to guard you in all your ways."

Ps. 106:34 "They did not destroy the peoples as the Lord had commanded them."

Ps. 107:11 " . . . because they rebelled against God's commands and despised the plans of the Most High."

Ps. 112:1   "Praise the Lord. Blessed are those who fear the Lord, who find great delight in his commands."

Ps. 119:19   "I am a stranger on earth; do not hide your <u>commands</u> from me."

Ps. 119:32   "I run in the path of your <u>commands</u>, for you have broadened my under-standing."

Ps. 119:35   "Direct me in the path of your <u>commands</u>, for there I find delight."

Ps. 119:48   "I reach out for your <u>commands</u>, which I love, that I may meditate on your decrees."

Ps. 119:86   "All your <u>commands</u> are trustworthy; help me, for I am being persecuted without cause."

Ps. 119:96   "To all perfection I see a limit, but your <u>commands</u> are boundless."

Ps. 119:98   "Your <u>commands</u> are always with me and make me wiser than my enemies."

Ps. 119:151   "Yet you are near, LORD, and all your <u>commands</u> are true."

Ps. 147:15   "He sends his <u>command</u> to the earth; his word runs swiftly."

Ps. 148:5   "Let them praise the name of the Lord, for at his <u>command</u> they were cre-ated."

a. Hebrew/Strong's/biblical use

- said, speak, tell
- to engage

b. Other versions/translations

- commandments
- counsel
- course
- directions
- gave the order
- give
- issued decree
- judgments
- ordered
- promises
- put
- tell, told
- words

c. Praise & Prayer Journal

1. Describe how God commanded creation in Genesis in six days, and His command to Adam and Eve.

2. Was God clear about His Ten Commandments given to Moses?

3. When were angels commanded? (Answers could include: Israelites crossing the Red Sea, announcing the birth of John the Baptist, announcing the birth of Jesus, warnings to Joseph about Jesus and Mary for their safety.)

4. What are other biblical examples of this characteristic, attribute, or action of God? (Answers could include: "Love the Lord your God and keep His commands always" [Deuteronomy 11:1]; "this calls for patience and endurance" on the part of the people of God who keep His commands and remain faithful to Jesus [Revelation 14:12].)

5. Have you received any commands from God? Have there been times He prompted or directed you and your path?

COMPASSIONATE: God is merciful, loves deeply, is slow to anger, is kind and tender, has tender love, has abundant mercies, has deep concern.

Ps. 51:1	"Have mercy on me, O God . . . according to your great <u>compassion</u> blot out my transgressions."
Ps. 86:15	"But you, LORD, are a <u>compassionate</u> and gracious God, slow to anger, abounding in love and faithfulness."
Ps. 103:4	" . . . who redeems your life from the pit and crowns you with love and <u>compassion</u>."
Ps. 103:8	"The LORD is <u>compassionate</u> and gracious, slow to anger, abounding in love."
Ps. 103:13	"As a father has <u>compassion</u> on his children, so the LORD has <u>compassion</u> on those who fear him."
Ps. 107:41	"But he <u>lifted the needy</u> out of their affliction and increased their families like flocks."
Ps. 111:4	"He has caused his wonders to be remembered; the LORD is gracious and <u>compassionate</u>."

Ps. 116:5   "The LORD is gracious and righteous; our God is full of <u>compassion</u>."

Ps. 119:156 "Your <u>compassion</u>, LORD, is great; preserve my life according to your laws."

Ps. 135:14   "For the LORD will vindicate his people and have <u>compassion</u> on his servants."

Ps. 145:9   "The LORD is good to all; he has <u>compassion</u> on all he has made."

Ps. 145:8   "The LORD is gracious and <u>compassionate</u>, slow to anger and rich in love."

a. Hebrew/Strong's/biblical use

- covenant: keeping loyalty, faithfulness, kindness, grace
- full of compassion, merciful
- loving kindness
- to love, love deeply, have mercy

b. Other versions/translations

- abundant mercy
- deep concern
- great compassion
- huge in mercy
- kind and tender
- merciful and gracious
- pities, pitieth
- sheer mercy
- showing sympathy
- tender love
- tender mercies
- to love deeply
- unlimited compassion
- your love

c. Praise & Prayer Journal

1. Who did God show compassion to in the Bible? (Answers include: Job, David, Jonah.)

2. What words are used multiple times along with compassionate? ("Gracious" is used five times in the Psalms along with compassion or compassionate; these are noted at the top of this chapter.)

3. What are biblical examples of this characteristic, attribute, or action of God? (Answers could include: The Lord God is compassionate [Exodus 34:6, Isaiah 30:18, Daniel 9:9, Joel 2:13]; The Lord will have compassion on His afflicted [Isaiah 49:13]; "For his compassions never fail" [Lamentations 3:22]; for the house of Judah and Joseph because "I have had compassion on them I will bring them back" [Zechariah 10:6].)

4. When has God exhibited His compassion and tender love toward you or others you know?

12   CONFRONTS: God meets, goes before, opposes, stands against, challenges face to face, makes somebody aware of something.

Ps. 17:13   "Rise up, LORD, <u>confront</u> them, bring them down; with your sword rescue me from the wicked."

a. Hebrew/Strong's/biblical use

- disappoint
- go before
- to meet, come, or be in front

b. Other versions/translations

- challenge somebody face to face
- encounter difficulty
- make somebody aware of something
- oppose
- stand against
- to pose a problem for someone

c. Praise & Prayer Journal

1. When did God and His power confront others in the Bible? (Answers could include: Adam and Eve, against Pharoah, the residents of and walls of Jericho, opposing the Philistines and their giant.)

2. What are other biblical examples of this characteristic, attribute, or action of God? (Scriptures include: God confronts with a sword, a flaming sword [Genesis 3:24];

"the sword of your majesty" [Deuteronomy 33:29]; a man was standing opposite him with his sword drawn [Joshua 5:13]; "arise, O Lord, save me" [Psalm 3:7]; God arises [Psalm 68:1]; those slain by the Lord [Isaiah 66:16]; a sword of the Lord [Jeremiah 47:16, Judges 7:20]; draw out a sword after them [Ezekiel 12:14].)

3. When have you observed that God confronted you or others or made you aware of something?

13 CONTENDS: God pleads my cause, stands up against others, opposes, defends, takes up and pleads my case, stands up for me, and is our advocate; He is in control.

Ps. 35:1   "Contend, Lord, with those who contend with me . . . "
Ps. 35:23 "Contend for me, my God and Lord."

a. Hebrew/Strong's/biblical use
- to plead, debate
- to strive, quarrel

b. Other versions/translations
- attack
- compete
- defend
- even unto my cause
- fight
- oppose
- plead my case
- plead my cause
- stand up against
- stand up for me
- state something
- struggle
- take up my case
- to and for my cause
- to deal with something

c. Praise & Prayer Journal
1. How did God contend with: the meetings between Pharaoh and Moses? Jericho? Jonah and the big fish?

2. How did God: Work with Abraham in protecting a few family members in Sodom and Gomorrah? Protect His people as the angel of death passed over them in Egypt? Work for Elijah in the test against the gods of Baal? Support Esther during her working with the king?

3. What are other biblical examples of this characteristic, attribute, or action of God? (Scriptures include: "the Lord said my spirit will not contend with humans forever" [Genesis 6:5]; "the Lord will fight for you" [Exodus 14:14].

4. When has God contended for you or your family members?

14 COUNSELS: God instructs, advises, guides, disciplines, provides wise counsel, gives good advice.

Ps. 16:7   "I will praise the LORD, who <u>counsels</u> me . . . "

Ps. 73:24   "You guide me with your <u>counsel</u> . . . "

a. Hebrew/Strong's/biblical use

- to advise
- to chasten, discipline, instruct, admonish
- to chastise (literally, with blows)

b. Other versions/translations

- admonish
- advises
- discipline
- gives me good advice
- guides
- wise counsel

c. Praise & Prayer Journal

1. What were the results after God counseled Abraham by establishing His covenant? Moses in dealing with His people? Joshua and David in their battles?

2. Describe examples of how the Spirit of God or the Holy Spirit counsels. (Examples could include: Solomon's wisdom, Ezekiel's visions, Daniel's dreams, the handwriting on the wall before Belshazzar, angels appearing, various signs.)

3. What are other biblical examples of this characteristic, attribute, or action of God? (Scriptures include: "I will counsel you with my eye upon you" [Psalm 32:8]; the counsel of the Lord stands forever [Psalm 33:11]; neglecting or not accepting God's counsel [Proverbs 1:25]; "great in counsel" [Jeremiah 32:19]; God counseled Jonah to go save the pagan Ninevites [Jonah 1].)

4. How has God counseled you and your family?

15

CREATOR: God establishes, makes, fashions, shapes, and forms; and He who has made us in His image, the image of God the Father, Son, and Holy Spirit.

Ps. 51:10   "<u>Create</u> in me a pure heart, O God, and renew a steadfast spirit within me."

Ps. 89:11   "The heavens are yours, and yours also the earth; you <u>founded</u> the world and all that is in it."

Ps. 89:12   "You <u>created</u> the north and the south . . . "

Ps. 90:2   "Before the mountains were born or you <u>brought forth</u> the whole world, from everlasting to everlasting you are God."

Ps. 95:6   "Come, let us bow down in worship, let us kneel before the Lord our <u>maker</u>."

a. Hebrew/Strong's/biblical use

- belong to you, you made
- to bear children, beget
- to create
- to do, make, accomplish, fashion
- to found, fix, establish, lay foundation
- to produce
- to shape, fashion, form

b. Other versions/translations

- fashion, shape, form
- formed
- gave birth
- make
- positioned
- to establish
- who made us

c. Praise & Prayer Journal

1. What did God create? (Among the answers: in six days, He made everything, the heavens and foundations of the earth [Genesis 1].)

2. What did God create that is unseen? (Possible answers: our DNA, our conscience, matter that holds the universe together, animal instincts, how plants are held in their places.)

3. Once a person is saved, how does God create a new person to replace the old?

4. What are other biblical examples of this characteristic, attribute, or action of God?

5. Has God created a new person and/or a pure heart in you and other members of your family?

16 CRUSHES: God breaks, shatters, strikes down, and destroys.

Ps. 10:10   "His victims are <u>crushed</u>, they collapse; they fall under his strength."

Ps. 18:38   "I <u>crushed</u> them so that they could not rise; they fell beneath my feet."

Ps. 44:2   " . . . you <u>crushed</u> the peoples . . . "

Ps. 44:19   "But you <u>crushed</u> us and made us a haunt for jackals; you covered us over with deep darkness."

Ps. 51:8   "Let me hear joy and gladness; let the bones you have <u>crushed</u> rejoice."

Ps. 72:4   " . . . may he <u>crush</u> the oppressor."

Ps. 89:10   "You <u>crushed</u> Rahab like one of the slain; with your strong arm you scattered your enemies."

Ps. 110:5   "He will <u>crush</u> kings on the day of his wrath."

a. Hebrew/Strong's/biblical use

- break (in pieces), bruise, to make contrite
- destroy, humble, oppress, smite
- to subdue or destroy
- pierce (through), smite, strike
- to beat to pieces
- to be broken
- to be shattered
- to bruise (literally or figuratively)
- to smite, shatter, wound severely
- wound

b. Other versions/translations

- beat
- beat others down
- beaten up
- break into pieces
- destroy
- execute
- shatter, shattered
- strike through
- strikes down
- struck
- to be broken
- wounded

c. Praise & Prayer Journal

1. How were Pharaoh's chariots crushed while they were chasing God's people passing through the parted Red Sea? How were the walls of Jericho crushed?

2. What are other biblical examples of this characteristic, attribute, or action of God? (Answers could include: Sodom and Gomorrah, various enemies of God's people, Samson in the temple.)

3. Have you ever observed God crushing ungodly enemies?

17

DEFENDS: God judges, punishes, condemns, vindicates, stands up for, brings justice, is an advocate; He takes my side, fights, pleads, brings to justice, and is a protector.

Ps. 10:18 " . . . <u>defending</u> the fatherless and the oppressed."

Ps. 68:5 "A father to the fatherless, a <u>defender</u> of widows."

Ps. 72:4 "He will <u>defend</u> the afflicted among the people."

Ps. 74:22 "Rise up, O God, and <u>defend</u> your cause; remember how fools mock you all day long."

Ps. 82:3 "<u>Defend</u> the cause of the weak and fatherless."

Ps. 119:154 "<u>Defend</u> my cause and redeem me; preserve my life according to your promise."

a. Hebrew/Strong's/biblical use

- a judge, advocate
- to judge, govern, vindicate, punish
- plead, condemn

b. Other versions/translations

- a champion
- a judge
- a protector
- an advocate
- argue
- bring justice
- fight
- give justice to
- plead
- stand up for
- take my side
- takes care of
- to bring justice to
- to judge, punish, condemn, vindicate
- to provide justice
- to vindicate

c. Praise & Prayer Journal

1. How did God's angels defend God's people as they were chased by Pharaoh's army before they reached the Red Sea? How did God defend Israel in the days of Gideon? Of other judges? How did David defend Israel against the Philistine giant, Goliath?

2. What are biblical examples of this characteristic, attribute, or action of God? (Answers could include: Naomi as a widower; defending David while Saul was pursuing him; Nehemiah when approaching the king with a plan to rebuild the walls of Jerusalem and temple; while Nehemiah and Israel were rebuilding, defending His people from neighboring enemies; Esther when she bravely approached the king to save God's people.)

3. When has God defended you and your family?

DELIVERS: God is our help and saves, reaches down, handles, rescues, answers, defends; helps provide an escape, a way to allow us to slip away and avert danger.

Ps. 3:7	"Arise, LORD! <u>Deliver</u> me, my God! Strike all my enemies on the jaw; break the teeth of the wicked."
Ps. 6:4	"Turn, LORD, and <u>deliver</u> me; save me because of your unfailing love."
Ps. 18:2	"The LORD is my rock, my fortress and my <u>deliverer</u>."
Ps. 18:43	"You have <u>delivered</u> me from the attacks of the people."
Ps. 22:4	"They trusted and you <u>delivered</u> them."
Ps. 22:8	"Let him <u>deliver</u> him, since he delights in him."
Ps. 22:20	"<u>Deliver</u> me from the sword . . ."
Ps. 34:4	"I sought the LORD, and he answered me; he <u>delivered</u> me from all my fears."
Ps. 34:7	"The angel of the LORD encamps around those who fear him, and He <u>delivers</u> them."

Ps. 34:17	"The righteous cry out, and the LORD hears them; he <u>delivers</u> them from all their troubles."
Ps. 34:19	"The righteous person may have many troubles, but the LORD <u>delivers</u> him from them all."
Ps. 37:40	"The LORD helps them and <u>delivers</u> them; he <u>delivers</u> them from the wicked and saves them."
Ps. 40:17	"You are my help and my <u>deliverer</u>; you are my God, do not delay."
Ps. 41:1	" . . . the LORD <u>delivers</u> them in times of trouble."
Ps. 50:15	" . . . and call on me in the day of trouble; I will <u>deliver</u> you, and you will honor me."
Ps. 54:7	"You have <u>delivered</u> me from all my troubles, and my eyes have looked in triumph on my foes."
Ps. 69:18	"Come near and rescue me; <u>deliver</u> me because of my foes."
Ps. 70:5	"You are my help and my <u>deliverer</u>; LORD, do not delay."
Ps. 71:2	"In your righteousness, rescue me and <u>deliver</u> me; turn your ear to me and save me."
Ps. 71:4	"<u>Deliver</u> me, my God, from the hand of the wicked, from the grasp of those who are evil and cruel."
Ps. 72:12	"For he will <u>deliver</u> the needy who cry out, the afflicted who have no one to help."
Ps. 79:9	"Help us, God our Savior . . . <u>deliver</u> us and forgive our sins for your name's sake."
Ps. 82:4	"Rescue the weak and the needy; <u>deliver</u> them from the hand of the wicked."
Ps. 97:10	"Let those who love the LORD hate evil, for he guards the lives of his faithful ones and <u>delivers</u> them from the hand of the wicked."
Ps. 107:6	" . . . he <u>delivered</u> them from their distress."
Ps. 107:28	"They cried out to the LORD in their trouble, and He brought them out from their distress."
Ps. 109:21	"Out of the goodness of your love, <u>deliver</u> me."

Ps. 119:170 "May my supplication come before you; <u>deliver</u> me according to your promise."

Ps. 144:7 "Reach down your hand from on high; <u>deliver</u> me and rescue me from the mighty waters, from the hands of foreigners."

Ps. 144:11 "<u>Deliver</u> me; rescue me from the hands of foreigners whose mouths are full of lies."

a. Hebrew/Strong's/biblical use

- arm for war
- escape, save, slip away
- remove, draw out, take off, withdraw
- to go out, exit, come out
- to save
- to ransom, rescue, deliver
- to return, turn back

b. Other versions/translations

- answers
- defends
- escapes
- freed
- frees
- got me out of
- grabs (to pull to safety)
- handles
- help
- helper
- helps
- my rescue
- my Savior
- ransoms
- reaches down
- redeems
- rescues
- saves
- snatches
- to save
- vindicates

c. Praise & Prayer Journal

1. Did God deliver Lot's family from wickedness in Sodom and Gomorrah (except for Lot's wife after departing)? Why was Lot's wife not saved?

2. Who else in the Bible was delivered from enemies? (Answers could include: Noah, Isaac from being sacrificed, Moses leading the Israelites out of Egypt, Joshua, David, all of God's people.)

3. What are other biblical examples of this characteristic, attribute, or action of God? (Among many possible answers: the Jewish people were delivered because of Esther's faith and courage in approaching and dealing with the king.)

4. Has God delivered you from your fears, troubles, distresses?

19   **DESPISES/DOES NOT DESPISE**: God does or does not reject, refuse, dismiss, or forget.

Ps. 53:5   "You put them to shame, for God <u>despised</u> them."

Ps. 69:33   "The LORD hears the needy and does not <u>despise</u> his captive people."

Ps. 102:17   "He will respond to the prayer of the destitute; he will not <u>despise</u> their plea."

a. Hebrew/Strong's/biblical use

- to hold in contempt, disdain
- to reject, despise, refuse

b. Other versions/translations

- hates them
- not dismiss
- not forget
- not reject
- not walk out
- refuse
- rejected them
- send them packing for good
- won't say no

c. Praise & Prayer Journal

1. What are biblical examples of this characteristic, attribute, or action of God? (Possible answers: God will not despise His captive people [the Israelites]; God will not despise the needy or destitute.)

2. When has God *not* rejected you at a time when you felt He might, or would? Other members of your family?

	DESTROYS: God perishes, tears down, tears away, puts to an end and takes away; He destroys wicked and evil people and those who tell lies.
20	

Ps. 5:6   "You <u>destroy</u> those who tell lies . . . "

Ps. 9:5   " . . . and <u>destroyed</u> the wicked."

Ps. 10:15   "<u>Break</u> the arm of the wicked and evil man . . . "

Ps. 28:5   "He will <u>tear</u> them down and never build them up again."

Ps. 50:22   "Consider this, you who forget God, or I will <u>tear</u> you to pieces with none to rescue."

Ps. 52:5   "Surely God will bring you down to everlasting ruin: He will . . . <u>tear</u> you from your tent . . . [and] <u>uproot</u> you."

Ps. 73:27   "Those who are far from you will perish; you <u>destroy</u> all who are unfaithful to you."

Ps. 78:38   "Yet he was merciful; he forgave their iniquities and did not <u>destroy</u> them. Time after time he restrained his anger and did not stir up his full wrath."

Ps. 145:20   "The Lord watches over all who love him, but all the wicked he will <u>destroy</u>."

a. Hebrew/Strong's/biblical use

- beat down, break through
- destroy, pluck down, pull down
- render, pluck
- rout
- tear away

- tear down, break down, overthrow
- throw down, ruin
- to break, break in pieces
- to perish

b. Other versions/translations

- afflicted
- destroyed evil people
- destroyed wicked people
- made the wicked perish
- permanently demolish
- put to an end
- rips

- sent those people packing
- smash them to smithereens
- take away, throw you out
- to perish
- to tear down

c. Praise & Prayer Journal

1. Name some times when God destroyed His enemies or the wicked. (Answers could include: the wicked before the great flood, except for Noah and his family; destroyed the plans of the Tower of Babel; Sodom and Gomorrah; the Egyptians; Jericho; the Philistines.)

2. What are other biblical examples of this characteristic, attribute, or action of God?

3. When have you been thankful that God did not destroy you or others because of sins but rather forgave iniquity and restrained His anger?

21 DISCIPLINES: God instructs, punishes, continues to punish, corrects, purges, rebukes, trains, and can rebuke and discipline anyone for their sin.

Ps. 6:1   "Lord, do not rebuke me in your anger or <u>discipline</u> me in your wrath."

Ps. 38:1   "O Lord, do not rebuke me in your anger or <u>discipline</u> me in your wrath."

Ps. 39:11   "When you rebuke and <u>discipline</u> anyone for their sin, you consume their wealth like a moth—surely everyone is but a breath."

Ps. 94:10   "Does he who <u>disciplines</u> nations not punish? Does he who teaches mankind lack knowledge?"

Ps. 94:12   "Blessed is the one you <u>discipline</u>, LORD, the one you teach from your law."

a. Hebrew/Strong's/biblical use

- to admonish with blows
- to chasten, instruct
- to chastise

b. Other versions/translations

- chasten
- chasteness
- chastiseth
- continue to punish
- correct

- instructs
- punish
- purge
- rebukes
- trains

c. Praise & Prayer Journal

1. Who did God discipline in the Bible? (Answers could include: Adam and Eve, Moses, Samson, David, Jonah.) What were the consequences of such discipline?

2. How has God disciplined entire nations? (Answers could include: Israel for forty years in the desert, the Egyptians, the Philistines, the Ninevites.)

3. What other biblical examples of this characteristic, attribute, or action of God can you name?

4. How have you or others you know been corrected, instructed, trained, or disciplined by God?

22

DWELLS: God sits enthroned (a place where He lives and inhabits); He is on His throne; He watches all.

Ps. 26:8   "LORD, I love the house where you live, the place where your glory <u>dwells</u>."

Ps. 33:14   "From His <u>dwelling</u> place He watches all who live on earth."

Ps. 46:4   "There is a river whose streams make glad the city of God, the holy place where the Most High <u>dwells</u>."

Ps. 85:9   "Surely his salvation is near those who fear him, that his glory may <u>dwell</u> in our land."

Ps. 90:1   "LORD, you have been our <u>dwelling</u> place throughout all generations."

Ps. 91:9   "If you make the Most High your <u>dwelling</u>—even the LORD, who is my refuge."

Ps. 135:21   "Praise be to the LORD from Zion, to him who <u>dwells</u> in Jerusalem."

a. Hebrew/Strong's/biblical use

- city
- dwell, remain, inhabit
- house, household
- refuge
- retreat, den, habitation
- settle down

b. Other versions/translations

- dwelleth
- filled, remain
- habitation
- He sits enthroned
- holy dwelling
- holy habitation
- home
- lives
- our refuge
- place where He lives
- seen, appear
- tabernacles of the Most High
- throne

c. Praise & Prayer Journal

1. How does the Bible describe the "City of God" where the Most High dwells?

2. How and where did God dwell in His people's land, and in Jerusalem?

3. How did God show His presence in the Ark of the Covenant as it was being carried by His people?

4. What are other biblical examples of this characteristic, attribute, or action of God? (Answers could include: the Holy of Holies, the tabernacle.)

5. In the New Testament, what are the conditions needed for the Holy Spirit to dwell in a person?

23 ENABLES: God adjusts, brings forth, and enables me.

Ps. 18:33   " . . . He <u>enables</u> me to stand on the heights."

a. Hebrew/Strong's/biblical use

- to adjust (i.e.: counterbalance, be suitable, compose, place, yield)
- to avail, behave, bring forth

b. Other versions/translations

- bring forth
- gives agility
- maketh, make, makes, made
- to adjust

c. Praise & Prayer Journal

1. How did God enable Joseph, Moses, and David?

2. What are other biblical examples of this characteristic, attribute, or action of God? (Example: Esther in approaching the king to save her people.)

3. How has God enabled you in your goals, dreams, or work?

4. How should you pray for God to enable yourself and others?

24 ENCOURAGES: God, specifically for the afflicted, establishes, prepares, strengthens, cheers up, and can provide a feeling of being secure.

Ps. 10:17   "You, Lord, hear the desire of the afflicted; you <u>encourage</u> them, and you listen to their cry."

a. Hebrew/Strong's/biblical use

- established
- prepared
- ready

- to be firm
- to be stable

b. Other versions/translations

- cheer them up
- established
- make feel secure
- make feeling secure

- prepare
- prepared
- strengthen

c. Praise & Prayer Journal

1. When did God encourage? (Answers could include: Noah, in building the ark; when He sent Moses to His people who were slaves in Egypt.)

2. What are other biblical examples of this characteristic, attribute, or action of God? (Answers could include: the judges, including Gideon in his defeat of the Midianites; through Jonathan, in his encouraging of David; through Mordecai, in his encouragement of Esther.)

3. When should we ask God to encourage us, and others, on our prayer list?

25 ENTHRONED: God sovereignly sits as King, is seated on the Judge's bench in His holy temple and dwelling.

Ps. 2:4   "The One <u>enthroned</u> in heaven laughs; the Lord scoffs at them."

Ps. 9:4   "For you have upheld my right and my cause, sitting <u>enthroned</u> as the righteous judge."

Ps. 9:7   "The Lord reigns forever; he has established his <u>throne</u> for judgment."

Ps. 11:4   " . . . the Lord is on his heavenly <u>throne</u>."

Ps. 22:3   "Yet you are <u>enthroned</u> as the Holy One . . . "

Ps. 29:10   "The Lord sits <u>enthroned</u> over the flood; the Lord is enthroned as king forever."

Ps. 45:6   "Your <u>throne</u>, O God, will last for ever and ever; a scepter of justice will be the scepter of your kingdom."

Ps. 47:8   "God reigns over the nations; God is seated on his holy <u>throne</u>."

Ps. 55:19   "God, who is <u>enthroned</u> from of old, who does not change—he will hear them and humble them, because they have no fear of God."

Ps. 80:1   " Hear us, Shepherd of Israel, you who lead Joseph like a flock. You who sit <u>enthroned</u> between the cherubim, shine forth."

Ps. 89:14   "Righteousness and justice are the foundation of Your <u>throne</u> . . . "

Ps. 89:36   " . . . that His line will continue forever and His <u>throne</u> endure before me like the sun."

Ps. 93:2   "Your <u>throne</u> was established long ago; you are from all eternity."

Ps. 97:2   "Clouds and thick darkness surround him; righteousness and justice are the foundation of his <u>throne</u>."

Ps. 99:1   "The Lord reigns, let the nations tremble; he sits <u>enthroned</u> between the cherubim, let the earth shake."

Ps. 102:12 "But you, LORD, sit <u>enthroned</u> forever; your renown endures through all generations."

Ps. 103:19 "The LORD has established his <u>throne</u> in heaven, and his kingdom rules over all."

Ps. 113:5 "Who is like the LORD our God, the One who sits <u>enthroned</u> on high?"

Ps. 123:1 "I lift up my eyes to you, to you who sit <u>enthroned</u> in heaven."

a. Hebrew/Strong's/biblical use

- dwell, remain, inhabit
- seated
- to sit, abide

b. Other versions/translations

- abides
- above it all
- dwell
- endure
- high throne
- holy temple
- inhabitant
- judge's bench
- on high
- remain
- rule
- sit as king
- sits, seated
- sovereign

c. Praise & Prayer Journal

1. Describe God's actions while being enthroned. (Answers could include: sitting, laughs, scoffs, hears, humbles.)

2. When was God's throne established? (Answers could include: from eternity, lasting forever.)

3. Describe God's throne. (Among the answers: heavenly, clouds, thick darkness.)

4. What are the foundations of His throne? (Among the answers: righteousness and justice.)

5. What are other biblical examples of this characteristic, attribute, or action of God? (Answers could include various visions by Isaiah, Daniel, Ezekiel.)

26

ETERNAL (FOREVER): God is everlasting, indefinite, unending, endless, permanently established, and dependable. God is immutable—never changing or varying; His very being is unchangeable.

Ps. 16:11	"You make known to me the path of life; you will fill me with joy in your presence, with <u>eternal</u> pleasures at your right hand."
Ps. 45:6	"Your throne, O God, will last <u>forever</u> and ever."
Ps. 89:2	I will declare that your love stands firm <u>forever</u>."
Ps. 89:4	"I will establish your line <u>forever</u> and make Your throne firm through all generations."
Ps. 89:36	" . . . that his line will continue <u>forever</u> and his throne endure before me like the sun."
Ps. 89:37	" . . . it will be established <u>forever</u> like the moon."
Ps. 90:1	"Lᴏʀᴅ, you have been our dwelling place <u>throughout all generations</u>."
Ps. 90:2	"Before the mountains were born . . . from <u>everlasting to everlasting</u>, you are God."
Ps. 102:12	"But you, O Lᴏʀᴅ, sit enthroned <u>forever</u>."
Ps. 111:10	"The fear of the Lᴏʀᴅ is the beginning of wisdom; all who follow his precepts have good understanding. To him belongs <u>eternal</u> praise."
Ps. 119:89	"Your word, Lᴏʀᴅ, is <u>eternal</u>; it stands firm in the heavens."
Ps. 119: 152	"Long ago I learned from your statutes that you established them to last <u>forever</u>."
Ps. 119:160	"All your words are true; all your righteous laws are <u>eternal</u>."

a. Hebrew/Strong's/biblical use

- ever, everlasting, perpetual, evermore, always
- indefinite, unending, future
- long duration, antiquity, futurity

- long time, forever
- perpetuity, continuing future

b. Other versions/translations

- beginning to end
- continues forever
- dependable
- endless
- endure
- endureth forever
- established
- eternal
- everlasting

- evermore
- firmly fixed
- forever, forevermore
- guaranteed life
- has always been
- here for good
- indefinite
- lasts forever
- permanent

- permanently established
- perpetuity
- remain stable
- settled
- stand forever
- stand secure
- stands firm
- unending

c. Praise & Prayer Journal

1. Specifically, what about God is eternal? (Answers could include: His words, His righteous laws, His line or people, His love.)

2. What are other biblical examples of this characteristic, attribute, or action of God? (Answers could include: The Word of God, God's laws, His covenant.)

3. What else is eternal besides God? (Among the answers: life after death, the new Heaven, Hell or Hades.)

27 **EXAMINES**: God proves, tests, puts to proof, studies, watches over, and studies carefully.

Ps. 11:4   "He observes everyone on earth; his eyes <u>examine</u> them."

Ps. 11:5   "The Lᴏʀᴅ <u>examines</u> the righteous . . ."

Ps. 17:3   "Though you probe my heart, though you <u>examine</u> me at night and test me . . ."

Ps. 26:2   "Test me, LORD, and try me, <u>examine</u> my heart and my mind."

a. Hebrew/Strong's/biblical use

- examine, try, prove
- to attend to, number, visit
- to smelt, refine

- to test, put to proof or test
- try, prove

b. Other versions/translations

- behold
- confronted me
- examines
- proves

- put to proof
- study
- study me carefully
- tests

- try, trieth
- visit
- watches over

c. Praise & Prayer Journal

1. Who does God examine? (Among the answers: me, everyone, the righteous, the wicked.)

2. When does God examine? (Among the answers: at night, all day, all the time.)

3. What does God examine? (Possible answers: heart, mind.)

4. What famous Bible characters provide examples of this characteristic, attribute, or action of God? (Answers could include: Job, Moses, Joshua, David, Daniel, Jeremiah, His people.)

5. Have you ever felt as though God has X-rayed you or your family's life?

28 FAITHFUL: God is loyal, love, trustworthy, keeps every promise and covenant, and is full of kindness.

Ps. 25:10   "All the ways of the LORD are loving and <u>faithful</u>."

Ps. 31:5   "Into your hands I commit my spirit; deliver me, LORD, my <u>faithful</u> God."

Ps. 33:4   "For the word of the Lᴏʀᴅ is right and true; He is <u>faithful</u> in all He does."

Ps. 36:5   " . . . your <u>faithfulness</u> to the skies."

Ps. 57:3   "God sends his love and his <u>faithfulness</u>."

Ps. 57:10   "For great is your love, reaching to the heavens; your <u>faithfulness</u> reaches to the skies."

Ps. 88:11   " . . . your <u>faithfulness</u> in destruction?"

Ps. 89:1   " . . . your <u>faithfulness</u> known through all generations."

Ps. 89:2   " . . . you established your <u>faithfulness</u> in heaven itself."

Ps. 89:5   " . . . your <u>faithfulness</u> too, in the assembly of the holy ones."

Ps. 89:8   " . . . your <u>faithfulness</u> surrounds you."

Ps. 89:14   " . . . love and <u>faithfulness</u> go before you."

Ps. 89:24   "My <u>faithful</u> love will be with him . . . "

Ps. 89:49   "O Lᴏʀᴅ, where is your former great love, which in your <u>faithfulness</u> you swore to David?"

Ps. 91:4   " . . . his <u>faithfulness</u> will be your shield and rampart."

Ps. 92:2   "Proclaim your love in the morning and your <u>faithfulness</u> at night."

Ps. 111:7   "The works of his hands are <u>faithful</u> and just; all his precepts are trustworthy."

Ps. 119:90   "Your <u>faithfulness</u> continues through all generations."

Ps. 145:13   "The Lᴏʀᴅ is <u>faithful</u> to all his promises and loving toward all he has made."

Ps. 146:6   "He is the maker of heaven and earth, the sea, and everything in them—he remains <u>faithful</u> forever."

a. Hebrew/Strong's/biblical use

- covenant-keeping loyalty
- faithfulness, kindness
- firmness, fidelity, steadfastness, steadiness
- grace, lovingkindness
- truth (as relates to faithfulness)

b. Other versions/translations

- fair
- faithfulness
- faithful pledge
- faithful presence
- faithful ways
- fidelity
- good

- He makes good on His word
- His Word
- keeps every promise
- loyal love
- loyalty
- promise

- reliable
- reliable oath
- trustworthy
- truth
- unfailing
- verify
- you never let me down

c. Praise & Prayer Journal

1. How has God been faithful to His people? (Individual examples include: His promises to Abraham, Jacob, Joseph, the Israelites' escape from Egypt, providing food in the desert, Ruth, Naomi.)

2. Name as many other biblical examples of this characteristic, attribute, or action of God as you can.

3. Do we underestimate how many ways God has been faithful to us and our families? Provide examples.

29 | **FATHER**: God is a heavenly Father, our advocate, and He has compassion on His children.

Ps. 2:7   "I will proclaim the LORD's decree: He said to me, 'You are my son; today I have become your <u>father</u>.'"

Ps. 68:5   "A <u>father</u> to the fatherless, a defender of widows, is God in his holy dwelling."

Ps. 89:26   "You are my <u>Father</u>, my God, the rock, my savior."

Ps. 103:13   "As a <u>father</u> has compassion on his children, so the LORD has compassion on those who fear him."

a. Hebrew/Strong's/biblical use

- Father: advocate
- Father: judge

b. Other versions/translations

- advocate
- begotten you
- "Today I became your father"

c. Praise & Prayer Journal

1. How special is it to have our heavenly God as a Father?

2. What are biblical examples of this characteristic, attribute, or action of God? (Answers could include: providing blessings to the fatherless and widows, such as Ruth.)

3. How has God been a loving, compassionate Father to you and your family?

30

FEARED: God is to be revered, honored, respected; He is awesome and watches over every move.

Ps. 76:7	"It is you alone who are to be <u>feared</u>. Who can stand before you when you are angry?"
Ps. 76:11	"Let all the neighboring lands bring gifts to the One to be <u>feared</u>."
Ps. 89:7	"In the council of the holy ones God is greatly <u>feared</u>."
Ps. 96:4	"For great is the LORD and most worthy of praise; he is to be <u>feared</u> above all gods."

a. Hebrew/Strong's/biblical use

- Object of reverence

- To honor, respect
- To revere, be afraid

b. Other versions/translations

- awesome One
- fierce you are
- honored
- more awesome than
- respected
- respect for you alone
- should have respect for

- stand in awe
- terrifying
- to revere
- who should be respected
- who watches our every move
- you are greatly feared

c. Praise & Prayer Journal

1. How should we honor and show our respect for God?

2. Whom did God show *why* He should be feared? (Answers could include: Pharaoh, the Egyptians, Philistines, Ninevites, Nebuchadnezzar, the Babylonians.)

3. What are other biblical examples of this characteristic, attribute, or action of God? (Possible answers: God's display in His contest against the gods of Baal through the prophet Elijah, Babylonian kings Nebuchadnezzar and Belshazzar in their encounters with God.)

4. What have been some of God's awesome actions toward you, your family, your ancestral line?

31 **FLOURISHER**: God can make you increase, continue to bless you, richly bless, give growth, and increase you more.

Ps. 44:2 " . . . and made our fathers <u>flourish</u>."

Ps. 115:14 "May the LORD cause you to <u>flourish</u>, both you and your children."

a. Hebrew/Strong's/biblical use

- continue to bless you
- enlarge
- increase you more
- make you increase
- richly bless
- to plant, fasten, fix, establish

b. Other versions/translations

- continue to bless
- gave all the land
- giving growth
- increase more
- increase your numbers
- planted, settled
- richly bless

c. Praise & Prayer Journal

1. Does God want us to flourish, increase, and be blessed? (Among the answers: yes, the prayer of Jabez.)

2. Who did God flourish in the Bible? (Among the numerous answers: Abraham, Isaac, Jacob [also known as Israel], Joseph, Job, Naomi, Ruth and Boaz, David, Jabez, Nehemiah.)

3. Who or what are other biblical examples of this characteristic, attribute, or action of God?

4. What are the many ways God has flourished you, your family, your job, your career, your business?

32 FORGIVES (BLOTS OUT): God pardons, wipes out, covers, purges, atones, gives a clean bill of health, and removes and wipes away the stains of sins.

Ps. 25:11   "For the sake of your name, Lord, <u>forgive</u> my iniquity, though it is great."

Ps. 51:1   " . . . <u>blot</u> out my transgressions."

Ps. 51:9   "Hide your face from my sins and <u>blot</u> out all my iniquity."

Ps. 79:9   "Help us, God our Savior, for the glory of your name; deliver us and <u>forgive</u> our sins for your name's sake."

Ps. 103:3   " . . . who <u>forgives</u> all your sins . . . "

a. Hebrew/Strong's/biblical use

- to cover, make atonement, purge
- to forgive, pardon
- to wipe, wipe out

b. Other versions/translations

- atones
- gives me a clean bill of health
- pardons
- provides atonement
- purge away

- removes
- removes the stain
- wipe away
- wipe out

c. Praise & Prayer Journal

1. Who was forgiven in the Bible? (Among the numerous answers: Adam and Eve, Abraham, Isaac, Jacob, Joseph, Joseph's brothers, Samson, David, Jonah.)

2. What are other biblical examples of this characteristic, attribute, or action of God?

3. Do your best to describe how blessed we are that God forgives, blots out, wipes out, and pardons our sins.

33

FORSAKES: While God for a time might leave, forsake, or abandon (example: Christ on the cross), He will never forsake His inheritance.

Ps. 9:10   " . . . for you, LORD, have never <u>forsaken</u> those who seek you."

Ps. 71:11   "They say, 'God has <u>forsaken</u> him; pursue him and seize him, for no one will rescue him.'"

Ps. 94:14   "For the LORD will not reject his people; he will never <u>forsake</u> his inheritance."

a. Hebrew/Strong's/biblical use

- Not leave, not forsake
- to leave, forsake
- to seek with care, inquire

b. Other versions/translations

- abandon, abandoned
- deserted
- inquire
- never deserted
- not abandon
- seek with care
- to leave

c. Praise & Prayer Journal

1. How can you be assured God will not forsake you? (Among the answers, from the Scriptures: He never forsakes those who seek Him; Matthew 28:20.)

2. How did God not abandon or desert his people in Egypt?

3. What are other biblical examples of this characteristic, attribute, or action of God? (Answers could include: Joseph, Job, David, Jonah, Jeremiah, Daniel.)

4. Have you ever felt as though God rejected you in the way the writer describes in Psalm 43:2?

5. Have you ever felt you or your family members were forsaken when, all along, He was there for you?

34

FORTRESS: God is a defense, strong place, place of safety and protection, refuge, strength, my rock, safe place, shelter, strong fort, and a saving defense.

Ps. 18:2   "The LORD is my rock and my <u>fortress</u> . . . "

Ps. 28:8   "The LORD is the strength of his people, a <u>fortress</u> of salvation for his anointed one."

Ps. 31:2   " . . . a strong <u>fortress</u> to save me."

Ps. 31:3   "Since you are my rock and my <u>fortress</u>, for the sake of your name lead and guide me."

Ps. 46:7   "The LORD Almighty is with us; the God of Jacob is our <u>fortress</u>."

Ps. 59:1   "Deliver me from my enemies, O God; be my <u>fortress</u> against those who are attacking me."

Ps. 59:9   "You are my strength, I watch for you; you, God, are my <u>fortress</u>."

Ps. 59:16   "I will sing of your love; for you are my <u>fortress</u>, my refuge in times of trouble."

Ps. 59:17   "You are my strength, I sing praise to you; you, God, are my <u>fortress</u>, my God on whom I can rely."

Ps. 62:2   "He alone is my rock and my salvation; he is my <u>fortress</u>, I will never be shaken."

Ps. 91:2   "I will say of the LORD, 'He is my refuge and my <u>fortress</u>, my God, in whom I trust.'"

Ps. 94:22   "The LORD has become my <u>fortress</u>."

Ps. 144:2   "He is my loving God and my <u>fortress</u>, my stronghold and my deliverer, my shield, in whom I take refuge, who subdues peoples under me."

a. Hebrew/Strong's/biblical use

- boldness, loud, might, majesty, praise, power, strength, strong
- a fastness, castle, defense, fort

- place or means of safety, protection, refuge, stronghold
- strength in various applications (force, security, majesty, praise)
- stronghold, strong place

b. Other versions/translations

- always count on you
- castle
- cave to hide in
- defend, defense
- deliverer
- fort
- hideout
- high mountain retreat
- house of defense
- impregnable castle
- like a fort to me
- mighty rock
- my place of safety

- my savior—
  my stronghold
- place of safety
- power
- protect, protector
- prowess
- refuge
- rock
- rock I go to for safety
- rock of protection/
  refuge/strength
- safe place
- salvation

- saving defense
- saving refuge
- shelter
- solid rock under my
  feet
- strength
- strong fort
- strong rock
- stronghold
- who saves me
- your granite cave,
  a hiding place

c. Praise & Prayer Journal

1. When did God provide a fortress? (Among the answers: for David, when Saul pursued him; for Daniel and his friends when the king threatened to kill all wise men in his court [Daniel 2]; for the apostle Paul, numerous times when his life was threatened.)

2. What are other biblical examples of this characteristic, attribute, or action of God? (Possible answers: Noah and the ark, pillar of fire protecting the Israelites, Daniel in the lion's den, Nehemiah.)

3. When have you been thankful that God was your rock (you can find this phrase three times in the Psalms list above) or fortress, saving defense, strength, stronghold?

35

GIVES: God accomplishes, provides, answers, delivers, enlightens, helps, pours down, rescues, restores, revives, saves, gives food to the hungry and to every creature, gives the desires of our hearts, and gives victories.

Ps. 13:3	"Look on me and answer, Lord my God. <u>Give</u> light to my eyes, or I will sleep in death."
Ps. 18:50	"He <u>gives</u> his king great victories . . . "
Ps. 20:4	"May he <u>give</u> you the desire of your heart . . . "
Ps. 20:6	"The Lord <u>gives</u> victory to his anointed."
Ps. 20:9	"Lord, <u>give</u> victory to the king! Answer us when we call!"
Ps. 21:1	"How great is his joy in the victories you <u>give</u>!"
Ps. 21:4	"He asked you for life, and you <u>gave</u> it to him."
Ps. 21:5	"Through the victories you <u>gave</u>, his glory is great."
Ps. 29:11	"The Lord <u>gives</u> strength to his people; the Lord blesses his people with peace."
Ps. 37:4	"Delight yourself in the Lord and he will <u>give</u> you the desires of your heart."
Ps. 44:7	" . . . but you <u>give</u> us victory over our enemies, you put our adversaries to shame."
Ps. 60:11	"<u>Give</u> us aid against the enemy, for human help is worthless."
Ps. 68:9	"You <u>gave</u> abundant showers, oh God."
Ps. 68:35	"You, God, are awesome in your sanctuary; the God of Israel <u>gives</u> power and strength to his people. Praise be to God!"
Ps. 71:3	"Be my rock of refuge, to which I can always go; <u>give</u> the command to save me, for you are my rock and my fortress."
Ps. 85:12	"The Lord will indeed <u>give</u> what is good, and our land will yield its harvest."
Ps. 104:27	"All look to you to <u>give</u> them their food at the proper time."

Ps. 108:12   "<u>Give</u> us aid against the enemy, for human help is worthless."

Ps. 119:73   "Your hands made me and formed me; <u>give</u> me understanding to learn your commands."

Ps. 119:130   "The unfolding of your words <u>gives</u> light; it gives understanding to the simple."

Ps. 119:143   "Trouble and distress have come upon me, but your commands <u>give</u> me delight."

Ps. 119:174   "I long for your salvation, Lord, and your law <u>gives</u> me delight."

Ps. 136:25   "He <u>gives</u> food to every creature."

Ps. 144:10   " . . . to the One who <u>gives</u> victory to kings, who delivers his servant David."

Ps. 146:7   "He upholds the cause of the oppressed and <u>gives</u> food to the hungry."

Ps. 146:8   "The Lord <u>gives</u> sight to the blind . . . "

a. Hebrew/Strong's/biblical use

- to do, make, accomplish, fashion
- to give, put, make
- to provide, ascribe, come
- a voluntary inclination, a freewill offering

b. Other versions/translations

- answer
- bestow
- brings
- deliver
- deliverance
- enlighten
- find
- grant, granted
- help, helped, helps
- imparts
- light up
- made it
- pours down
- provides
- rescues
- restore
- revive
- saves, saved
- surely give
- to accomplish
- your salvation

c. Praise & Prayer Journal

1. Who did God give to in the Bible? (Among the numerous answers, for God gave to everyone in the Bible in one way or another: Abraham, Jacob, Joseph, Joshua.)

2. What are other biblical examples of this characteristic, attribute, or action of God? (Answers could include: guiding the Israelites through the Exodus, Hannah, Job, David, Zechariah and Elizabeth.)

3. What has God given you and your family in the way of victories (you can see this phrase used seven times in the Psalms above), the desires of your heart (two times above), and/or strength, aid, power, what is good, insight, understanding, delight?

4. Do you specifically pray for God to answer your prayers, grant your requests, help you, and provide what is good?

36

GLORIOUS: God is majestic, magnificent, abundant, has splendor, and is to be honored.

Ps. 8:1	"LORD, our LORD, how majestic is your name in all the earth! You have set your <u>glory</u> in the heavens."
Ps. 19:1	"The heavens declare the <u>glory</u> of God; the skies proclaim the work of his hands."
Ps. 24:8	"Who is the King of <u>glory</u>? The LORD strong and mighty, the LORD mighty in battle."
Ps. 29:3	"The God of <u>glory</u> thunders, the LORD thunders over the mighty waters."
Ps. 57:5	"Be exalted, O God, above the heavens; let your <u>glory</u> be over all the earth."
Ps. 85:9	"Surely his salvation is near those who fear him, that his <u>glory</u> may dwell in our land."
Ps. 87:3	"<u>Glorious</u> things are said of you, city of God."
Ps. 96:6	"Splendor and majesty are before him; strength and <u>glory</u> are in his sanctuary."

Ps. 105:3	"<u>Glory</u> in his holy name; let the hearts of those who seek the LORD rejoice."
Ps. 111:3	"<u>Glorious</u> and majestic are his deeds, and his righteousness endures forever."
Ps. 115:1	"Not to us, LORD, not to us, but to your name be the <u>glory</u>, because of your love and faithfulness."
Ps. 106:20	"They exchanged their <u>glorious</u> God for an image of a bull, which eats grass."
Ps. 138:5	"May they sing of the ways of the LORD, for the <u>glory</u> of the LORD is great."
Ps. 145:5	"They speak of the <u>glorious</u> splendor of your majesty."
Ps. 145:12	" . . . so that all people may know of your mighty acts and the <u>glorious</u> splendor of your kingdom."

a. Hebrew/Strong's/biblical use

- abundance
- honor
- magnificent
- ornament, honor
- to be rich, be honorable, be honored

b. Other versions/translations

- abundance
- honorable
- lavish
- magnificent
- splendid, splendor
- to be rich

c. Praise & Prayer Journal

1. What is glorious? (Answers include: God, His heavens, His holy name, His sanctuary, His deeds, His splendor.)

2. Who did God disclose His glory to? (Answers include: Moses, Joshua, David, Solomon, Mary the mother of Jesus.)

3. What are other biblical examples of this characteristic, attribute, or action of God,

including His *majesty* or being *majestic* (the phrase is used three times in the Psalms above)? (Answers could include: Creation, at the parting of the Red Sea, Moses with God on Mount Sinai.)

4. How do you and your family give honor to God's glory, and how often do you do so?

37 **GOOD**: God repays, rewards, is excellent, is appropriate, has beauty, is prosperous, is merciful, kind, fair, plans only the best for me; we are blessed to experience the Lord's favor, so full of answered prayers.

Ps. 13:6   "I will sing to the LORD, for he has been <u>good</u> to me."

Ps. 16:2   " . . . apart from you I have no <u>good</u> thing."

Ps. 25:7   "Remember not the sins of my youth . . . according to your love remember me, for you are <u>good</u>."

Ps. 25:8   "<u>Good</u> and upright is the LORD . . . "

Ps. 27:13 "I am still confident of this: I will see the <u>goodness</u> of the LORD in the land of the living."

Ps. 34:8   "Taste and see that the LORD is <u>good</u>."

Ps. 69:16 "Answer me, O LORD, out of the <u>goodness</u> of your love."

Ps. 73:1   "Surely God is <u>good</u> to Israel, to those who are pure in heart."

Ps. 84:11 "No <u>good</u> thing does he withhold from those whose walk is blameless."

Ps. 85:12 "The LORD will indeed give what is <u>good</u>, and our land will yield its harvest."

Ps. 86:5   "You, LORD, are forgiving and <u>good</u>, abounding in love to all who call to you."

Ps. 100:5 "For the LORD is <u>good</u> and his love endures forever; his faithfulness continues through all generations."

Ps. 106:1   "Praise the LORD. Give thanks to the LORD, for he is <u>good</u>; his love endures forever."

Ps. 119:68   "You are <u>good</u>, and what you do is good; teach me your decrees."

Ps. 125:4   "LORD, do <u>good</u> to those who are <u>good</u>, to those who are upright in heart."

Ps. 136:1   "Give thanks to the LORD, for he is <u>good</u>."

Ps. 143:10   "Teach me to do your will, for you are my God; may your <u>good</u> Spirit lead me on level ground."

Ps. 145:9   "The LORD is <u>good</u> to all; he has compassion on all he has made."

a. Hebrew/Strong's/biblical use

- appropriate and becoming
- beauty or prosperity
- best part or best of anything
- good things, goodness, kindness
- goodness of intelligence, good understanding
- pleasant, agreeable, excellent
- reward, bestowed
- to deal fully with, recompense, repay
- uprightness, kindness

b. Other versions/translations

- dealt bountifully with me
- experience the Lord's favor
- extend to me your favor
- fair
- how good God is
- kind
- merciful
- plan only the best for me
- repay, reward
- so full of answered prayers
- vindicates me
- well being

c. Praise & Prayer Journal

1. How blessed are we that: God rewards? God is kind? His good Spirit leads us to level ground?

2. Why should we be thankful that God is good (and not bad) toward us, and that God is good to those whose walk is blameless and who are upright in heart?

3. What are biblical examples of this characteristic, attribute, or action of God? (Numerous answers could include: Noah, Noah's family, Abraham, Isaac, Jacob, Joseph, Ruth, Naomi, Zechariah and Elizabeth, Mary and Joseph, Mary Magdalene.)

4. How has God been good to you and your family?

38 GRACIOUS: God is full of grace, mercy, deep love, tender affection, holiness, kindness, and shows us His favor.

Ps. 67:1   "May God be <u>gracious</u> to us and bless us and make His face to shine upon us."

Ps. 86:15   "But you, O LORD, are a compassionate and <u>gracious</u> God."

Ps. 103:8   "The LORD is compassionate and <u>gracious</u>, slow to anger, abounding in love."

Ps. 116:5   "The LORD is <u>gracious</u> and righteous; our God is full of compassion."

Ps. 119:29 "Keep me from deceitful ways; be <u>gracious</u> to me and teach me your law."

Ps. 145:8   "The LORD is <u>gracious</u> and compassionate, slow to anger and rich in love."

a. Hebrew/Strong's/biblical use

- covenant: keeping loyalty, faithfulness, kindness, grace, lovingkindness
- have tender affection
- mercy, merciful
- to give to someone, anything, doing so graciously
- to have mercy on
- to love, love deeply
- to show favor, pity

b. Other versions/translations

- be merciful
- grace
- have pity on us
- holy and kind
- kind

- love deeply
- mark us with grace
- mercy, merciful
- show us his favor
- tender and kind

c. Praise & Prayer Journal

1. How has God been: compassionate (used four times in the Psalms above) to you, merciful to you, kind to you, and/or showed you His favor?

2. Explain how God is *both* gracious and compassionate.

3. What are biblical examples of this characteristic, attribute, or action of God? (Answers could include: Abraham and Sarah, Isaac and Rebekah, Jacob and wives Rachel and Leah, Joseph, Rahab, the Israelites preserved in the exile.)

4. How has God been gracious, or shown grace, to you and your family?

39

GRANTS: God fills, fulfills, brings, strengthens, and protects; and He can grant us support, success, relief, and peace.

Ps. 20:2	"May he send you help from the sanctuary and <u>grant</u> you support from Zion."
Ps. 20:5	"May the LORD <u>grant</u> all your requests."
Ps. 21:2	"You have <u>granted</u> him the desire of his heart."
Ps. 21:6	"Surely you have <u>granted</u> him eternal blessings."
Ps. 94:13	"You <u>grant</u> them relief from days of trouble, till a pit is dug for the wicked."
Ps. 118:25	"LORD, save us! LORD, <u>grant</u> us success!"

Ps. 127:2   "In vain you rise early and stay up late, toiling for food to eat—for he <u>grants</u> sleep to those he loves."

Ps. 147:14   "He <u>grants</u> peace to your borders and satisfies you with the finest of wheat."

a. Hebrew/Strong's/biblical use

- deliver, made
- dispatch
- to fill, be full
- to give, put, set

- to make
- to set, direct, direct toward
- to set, ordain, establish, bring to pass
- to put, set, lay, put or lay upon

b. Other versions/translations

- brings
- endowed
- fulfill, to fill
- give aid
- give you
- given, gave
- given, gave, giveth, gives
- keeps
- made, make, makes, maketh

- piled
- protects
- provides
- send now
- sends
- strengthen
- supplies
- support

c. Praise & Prayer Journal

1. How thankful are you that God can give, deliver, dispatch, set, direct, make, provide, send, and supply so many blessings?

2. What are biblical examples of this characteristic, attribute, or action of God? (Answers could include: Adam and Eve, Abraham's journey, Abraham and Sarah to have a child, Moses, Joshua, Ruth, Solomon, Zechariah and Elizabeth, Mary and Joseph.)

3. How has God granted you and your family support, your requests, the desires of your heart, eternal blessings, relief, success, sleep, peace?

40

GREAT: God is abundant, awesome, powerful, mighty, magnificent, marvelous, spectacular, unfailing, unlimited, wonderful, and He is supreme.

Ps. 17:7   "Show me the wonders of your <u>great</u> love, you who save by your right hand those who take refuge in you from their foes."

Ps. 25:6   "Remember, LORD, your <u>great</u> mercy and love, for they are from of old."

Ps. 33:16   "No king is saved by the size of his army; no warrior escapes by his <u>great</u> strength."

Ps. 47:2   "For the LORD Most High is awesome, the <u>great</u> King over all the earth."

Ps. 48:1   "<u>Great</u> is the LORD, and most worthy of praise, in the city of our God, his holy mountain."

Ps. 51:1   "Have mercy on me, O God, according to your unfailing love; according to your <u>great</u> compassion blot out my transgressions."

Ps. 57:10   "For <u>great</u> is your love, reaching to the heavens; your faithfulness reaches to the skies."

Ps. 69:16   "Answer me, LORD, out of the goodness of your love; in your <u>great</u> mercy turn to me."

Ps. 71:19   "Your righteousness, God, reaches to the heavens, you who have done <u>great</u> things. Who is like you, God?"

Ps. 77:13   "Your ways, God, are holy. What god is as <u>great</u> as our God?"

Ps. 86:10   "For you are <u>great</u> and do marvelous deeds; you alone are God."

Ps. 86:13   "For <u>great</u> is your love toward me; you have delivered me from the depths, from the realm of the dead."

Ps. 90:11   "If only we knew the power of your anger! Your wrath is as <u>great</u> as the fear that is your due."

Ps. 92:5   "How <u>great</u> are your works, O LORD, how profound your thoughts."

Ps. 95:3	"For the LORD is the <u>great</u> God, the <u>great</u> King above all gods."
Ps. 99:3	"Let them praise your <u>great</u> and awesome name—[you are] holy."
Ps. 117:2	"For <u>great</u> is his love towards us . . . "
Ps. 135:5	"I know that the LORD is <u>great</u>, that our LORD God is greater than all gods."
Ps. 147:5	"<u>Great</u> is our LORD and mighty in power; his understanding has no limit."

a. Hebrew/Strong's/biblical use

- mighty
- multitude, abundance
- strength, power, might

b. Other versions/translations

- abundant, awesome
- best
- lasting a long time
- magnificent
- marvelous, milestones, much, majestic
- much
- multitude, mighty
- powerful
- spectacular
- steadfast
- tender
- unfailing, unlimited
- very good
- wonderful

c. Praise & Prayer Journal

1. What great things did God do throughout biblical history? (Answers could include: the creation, the great flood, the Israelites' escape from Egypt, parting of the Red Sea, food and provisions in the desert for forty years, the fallen walls of Jericho, the saving of Daniel and his three friends numerous times, His working through Jonah, Mary's conception.)

2. What are other biblical examples of this characteristic, attribute, or action of God?

3. Specifically, what is great about God? Think of His love, mercy, strength, kingship, Lordship, compassion, and works?

4. Describe how God is supreme, superior, and highest in rank, power, and all thoughts.

5. Psalm 103:2-5 says we should not forget all His benefits, as one who forgives all our sins and heals all our diseases. Specifically, how can we do that?

6. How has God shown His greatness to you and your family?

41

GUARDS: God keeps us safe, protects, preserves, and takes good care of; and He guards the lives of His faithful ones.

Ps. 25:20   "<u>Guard</u> my life and rescue me; do not let me be put to shame, for I take refuge in you."

Ps. 86:2   "<u>Guard</u> my life, for I am faithful to you; save your servant, who trusts in you."

Ps. 91:11   "For he will command his angels concerning you to <u>guard</u> you in all your ways."

Ps. 97:10   "Let those who love the LORD hate evil, for he <u>guards</u> the lives of his faithful ones and delivers them from the hand of the wicked."

a. Hebrew/Strong's/biblical use

• keep, observe

b. Other versions/translations

• keep watch, keep, keeps safe
• protects, preserve
• take good care

c. Praise & Prayer Journal

1. How blessed are we that God guards, keeps watch over, keeps safe, and protects our lives?

2. What are biblical examples of this characteristic, attribute, or action of God? (Answers include: Noah and the ark, Abraham as he and his family left his homeland, Naomi and Ruth, David numerous times while being pursued by Saul, David in numerous battles, Daniel in the lion's den and other times he was rescued by God, Esther.)

3. How has God guarded and protected you and your family in your home, travels, work, sports, and hobbies?

42 GUIDES (LEADS): God directs, shows, sends, takes me by the hand, leads us in righteousness and in straight paths.

Ps. 5:8 "Lead me, LORD, in your righteousness because of my enemies—make your way straight before me."

Ps. 23:3 "He guides me in paths of righteousness for His name's sake."

Ps. 25:5 "Guide me in your truth and teach me, for you are God my Savior, and my hope is in you all day long."

Ps. 25:9 "He guides the humble in what is right and teaches them his way."

Ps. 27:11 ". . . lead me in a straight path."

Ps. 31:3 "Since you are my rock and my fortress, for the sake of your name lead and guide me."

Ps. 43:3 "Send forth your light and your truth, let them guide me."

Ps. 48:14 ". . . [God] will be our guide even to the end."

Ps. 67:4 "May the nations be glad and sing for joy, for you rule the peoples with equity and guide the nations of the earth."

Ps. 73:24 "You guide me with your counsel, and afterward you will take me into glory."

Ps. 139:10 ". . . even there your hand will guide me, your right hand will hold me fast."

a. Hebrew/Strong's/biblical use

- conduct
- to drive, lead away, carry away
- to lead, guide, to transport

b. Other versions/translations

- direct
- give me a map
- govern
- lead
- sends
- shows
- take me by the hand
- tend

c. Praise & Prayer Journal

1. When does God guide and lead in righteousness? (Answers could include: two times in the Psalms above, in truth, the humble, entire nations, with His counsel in straight paths.)

2. In the Bible, when did God guide and lead, but *not* in a straight path? (Answers could include: when His people rebelled and lacked faith and therefore wandered in the desert for forty years.)

3. What are other biblical examples of this characteristic, attribute, or action of God?

4. How has God guided, led, directed, or sent you and your family?

43 **HEALS**: God makes us healthy and restores my health.

Ps. 6:2   "O Lord, <u>heal</u> me, for my bones are in agony."

Ps. 30:2   " . . . and you <u>healed</u> me."

Ps. 41:4   " . . . <u>heal</u> me, for I have sinned against you."

Ps. 103:3   " . . . <u>heals</u> all your diseases."

Ps. 107:20   "He sent out his word and <u>healed</u> them; he rescued them from the grave."

Ps. 147:3   "He <u>heals</u> the brokenhearted and binds up their wounds."

a. Hebrew/Strong's/biblical use

- make healthy

b. Other versions/translations

- puts me together
- restores my health

c. Praise & Prayer Journal

1. Who was brokenhearted in the Bible but healed by God? (Answers could include: Hagar, Sarah's handmaiden, Job, Hannah, David.)

2. Has God healed your brokenheartedness?

3. What are other biblical examples of this characteristic, attribute, or action of God?

4. When and how has God healed you and your family, or is healing you now?

44	**HEARS**: God answers, responds, listens, bows down His ear, bends an ear, listens closely, pays special attention, and is responsive.

Ps. 4:1   "... and <u>hear</u> my prayer."

Ps. 4:3   "Know that the Lord has set apart his faithful servant for himself; the Lord <u>hears</u> when I call to him."

Ps. 5:2   "<u>Hear</u> my cry for help, my King and my God, for to you I pray."

Ps. 5:3   "In the morning, O Lord, you <u>hear</u> my voice . . . "

Ps. 6:8   "... for the Lord has <u>heard</u> my weeping."

Ps. 6:9   "The LORD has <u>heard</u> my cry for mercy."

Ps. 10:17   "You, LORD, <u>hear</u> the desire of the afflicted; you encourage them, and you listen to their cry."

Ps. 17:1   "<u>Hear</u> me, LORD, my plea is just; listen to my cry. Hear my prayer—it does not rise from deceitful lips."

Ps. 17:6   "I call on you, my God, for you will answer me; turn your ear to me and <u>hear</u> my prayer."

Ps. 18:6   "From his temple he <u>heard</u> my voice; my cry came before him, into his ears."

Ps. 27:7   "<u>Hear</u> my voice when I call, LORD; be merciful to me and answer me."

Ps. 28:2   "<u>Hear</u> my cry for mercy as I call to you for help, as I lift up my hands toward your Most Holy Place."

Ps. 28:6   "Praise be to the LORD, for he has <u>heard</u> my cry for mercy."

Ps. 30:10   "<u>Hear</u>, LORD, and be merciful to me; LORD, be my help."

Ps. 31:22   "Yet you <u>heard</u> my cry for mercy when I called to you for help."

Ps. 34:6   "This poor man called, and the LORD <u>heard</u> him."

Ps. 34:17   "The righteous cry out, and the LORD <u>hears</u> them."

Ps. 39:12   "<u>Hear</u> my prayer, LORD, listen to my cry for help; do not be deaf to my weeping."

Ps. 40:1   "I waited patiently for the LORD; he turned to me and <u>heard</u> my cry."

Ps. 54:2   "<u>Hear</u> my prayer, O God; listen to the words of my mouth."

Ps. 55:17   "Evening, morning, and noon I cry out in distress, and he <u>hears</u> my voice."

Ps. 55:19   "God, who is enthroned from old, who does not change—he will <u>hear</u> them and humble them, because they have no fear of God."

Ps. 61:1   "<u>Hear</u> my cry, O God; listen to my prayer."

Ps. 61:5   "For you, God, have <u>heard</u> my vows; you have given me the heritage of those who fear your name."

Ps. 64:1	"<u>Hear</u> me, my God, as I voice my complaint; protect my life from the threat of the enemy."
Ps. 69:33	"The Lord <u>hears</u> the needy and does not despise his captive people."
Ps. 77:1	"I cried out to God for help; I cried out to God to <u>hear</u> me."
Ps. 78:59	"When God <u>heard</u> them, he was furious; he rejected Israel completely."
Ps. 84:8	"<u>Hear</u> my prayer, Lord God Almighty; listen to me, God of Jacob."
Ps. 86:1	"<u>Hear</u> me, Lord, and answer me, for I am poor and needy."
Ps. 86:6	"<u>Hear</u> my prayer, Lord; listen to my cry for mercy."
Ps. 94:9	"Does he who fashioned the ear not <u>hear</u>? Does he who formed the eye not see?"
Ps. 97:8	"Zion <u>hears</u> and rejoices and the villages of Judah are glad because of your judgments, Lord."
Ps. 102:1	"<u>Hear</u> my prayer, Lord; let my cry for help come to you."
Ps. 106:44	"He took note of their distress when he <u>heard</u> their cry."
Ps. 116:1	"I love the Lord, for he <u>heard</u> my voice; he <u>heard</u> my cry for mercy."
Ps. 130:2	"Lord, <u>hear</u> my voice. Let your ears be attentive to my cry for mercy."
Ps. 140:6	"I say to the Lord, 'You are my God.' <u>Hear</u>, Lord, my cry for mercy."
Ps. 141:1	"I call to you, Lord, come quickly to me; <u>hear</u> me when I call to you."
Ps. 143:1	"Lord, <u>hear</u> my prayer, listen to my cry for mercy; in your faithfulness and righteousness come to my relief."
Ps. 145:19	"He fulfills the desires of those who fear him; he <u>hears</u> their cry and saves them."

a. Hebrew/Strong's/biblical use

- be attentive, heed
- listen, obey
- to answer, respond

b. Other versions/translations

- bow down thine ear, bend an ear
- give attention, gives ear, gave ear
- heed
- incline your ear
- know

- listens, listen closely
- open his ears to hear
- pay attention, paid special attention
- responds

c. Praise & Prayer Journal

1. When does God hear our cry? (Answers include: morning, noon, evening, through the watches of the night.)

2. Who does God hear? (Answers: the needy, the afflicted, the poor, the brokenhearted.)

3. What kinds of pleas does God hear? (Answers: our prayers [listed eight times in the Psalms above], our cries [listed five times in the Psalms], our cries for mercy [listed seven times in the Psalms], our cries for help, complaints, vows, and our voice [listed twice in the Psalms above].)

4. What are biblical examples of this characteristic, attribute, or action of God? (Answers include: God's people in captivity, Job, David's prayers and psalms.)

5. When has God heard and answered your prayers? The prayers of your family?

45 **HELPS**: God supports, aids, rescues, defends, helps, runs to my side, and powerfully puts me back on my feet.

Ps. 5:2   "Hear my cry for <u>help</u>, my king and my God."

Ps. 10:14	" . . . You are the <u>helper</u> of the fatherless."
Ps. 18:6	"In my distress I called to the Lord; I cried to my God for <u>help</u>. From his temple he heard my voice; my cry came before him, into his ears."
Ps. 18:29	"With your <u>help</u> I can advance against a troop . . . I can scale a wall."
Ps. 18:35	"You make your saving help my shield, and your right hand sustains me; your <u>help</u> has made me great."
Ps. 20:2	"May he send you <u>help</u> from the sanctuary . . . "
Ps. 22:19	"But you, Lord, do not be far from me. You are my strength; come quickly to <u>help</u> me."
Ps. 27:9	" . . . you have been my <u>helper</u>."
Ps. 28:7	" . . . my heart trusts in him, and he <u>helps</u> me."
Ps. 30:2	"Lord my God, I called to you for <u>help</u>, and you healed me."
Ps. 30:10	"Hear, Lord, and be merciful to me; Lord, be my <u>help</u>."
Ps. 33:20	"We wait in hope for the Lord; he is our <u>help</u> and our shield."
Ps. 37:40	"The Lord <u>helps</u> them and delivers them."
Ps. 38:22	"Come quickly to <u>help</u> me, my Lord and my Savior."
Ps. 40:13	" . . . come quickly, Lord, to <u>help</u> me."
Ps. 40:16	"But may all who seek you rejoice and be glad in you; may those who long for your saving <u>help</u> always say, 'The Lord is great!'"
Ps. 40:17	"You are my <u>help</u> and my deliverer."
Ps. 44:26	"Rise up and <u>help</u> us; rescue us because of your unfailing love."
Ps. 46:1	"God is our refuge and strength, an ever-present <u>help</u> in trouble."
Ps. 54:4	"Surely God is my <u>help</u>; the Lord is the one who sustains me."
Ps. 56:9	"Then my enemies will turn back when I call for <u>help</u>. By this I will know that God is for me."
Ps. 60:5	"Save us and <u>help</u> us with your right hand."
Ps. 63:7	"Because you are my <u>help</u>, I sing in the shadow of your wings."
Ps. 70:1	"Hasten, O God, to save me; come quickly, Lord, to <u>help</u> me."

Ps. 70:4	"But may all who seek you rejoice and be glad in you; may those who long for your saving <u>help</u> always say, 'The Lord is great!'"
Ps. 70:5	"You are my <u>help</u> and my deliverer."
Ps. 71:12	"Do not be far from me, my God; come quickly, God, to <u>help</u> me."
Ps. 79:9	"<u>Help</u> us, God our Savior, for the glory of your name; deliver us and forgive our sins for your name's sake."
Ps. 86:17	". . . for you, O Lord, have <u>helped</u> me and comforted me."
Ps. 88:13	"But I cry to you for <u>help</u>, Lord . . ."
Ps. 102:1	"Lord, let my cry for <u>help</u> come to you."
Ps. 108:6	"Save us and <u>help</u> us with your right hand, that those you love may be delivered."
Ps. 115:10	". . . trust in the Lord—he is their <u>help</u> and shield."
Ps. 115:11	"You who fear him, trust in the Lord—he is their <u>help</u> and shield."
Ps. 118:7	"The Lord is with me; he is my <u>helper</u>."
Ps. 118:13	"I was pushed back and about to fall, but the Lord <u>helped</u> me."
Ps. 121:2	"My <u>help</u> comes from the Lord, the maker of heaven and earth."

a. Hebrew/Strong's/biblical use

- aid
- assistance
- one who helps, delivers, defends
- rescue
- to deliver
- to help, support

b. Other versions/translations

- aid, assistance
- defend, deliver
- for by you
- helper
- not let them down
- powerfully put me back on my feet
- reinforcements rescued
- run to my side
- strength
- way

c. Praise & Prayer Journal

1. Who does God help? (Answers include: me [seven times in the Psalms list above], my help [seven times in the Psalms list], you, us [four times in the Psalms list].)

2. When does God help? (Answers include: when one who loves Him is in trouble, facing an enemy, in danger; He puts us back on our feet when we stumble, trip, or fall.)

3. What are biblical examples of this characteristic, attribute, or action of God? (Among numerous answers: Noah, Hagar, Joseph, Moses, Rahab, Job, David, Daniel and his three friends [Daniel 2], Daniel in the lion's den [Daniel 6].)

4. Do you *actively know* that God is your helper?

5. Do we fail to pray for God's help?

6. When did God help you, your family, your friends?

46

HIDES: God allows us to hide in His shelter; at times He seems to be concealed, hidden, in secret, avoiding me like being cut off, paying no attention to me, or as one who stands far off or away.

Ps. 10:1	"Why, Lord, do you stand far off? Why do you <u>hide</u> yourself in times of trouble?"
Ps. 13:1	"How long, Lord? Will you forget me forever? How long will you <u>hide</u> your face from me?"
Ps. 27:5	"For in the day of trouble he will keep me safe in his dwelling; he will <u>hide</u> me in the shelter of his sacred tent and set me high upon a rock."
Ps. 31:20	"In the shelter of your presence you <u>hide</u> them from all human intrigues; you keep them safe in your dwelling from accusing tongues."
Ps. 38:9	"All my longings lie open before you, Lord; my sighing is not <u>hidden</u> from you."
Ps. 64:2	"<u>Hide</u> me from the conspiracy of the wicked, from the plots of evildoers."

Ps. 69:5   "You, God, know my folly; my guilt is not <u>hidden</u> from you."

Ps. 88:14   "Why, LORD, do you reject me and <u>hide</u> your face from me?"

Ps. 89:46   "How long, LORD? Will you <u>hide</u> yourself forever? How long will your wrath burn like fire?"

Ps. 102:2   "Do not <u>hide</u> your face from me when I am in distress. Turn your ear to me; when I call, answer me quickly."

a. Hebrew/Strong's/biblical use

- be concealed, be secret
- to conceal, hide, be hidden
- to cut off, cut down, destroy, make desolate, kick
- to hide, to conceal

b. Other versions/translations

- avoiding me
- conceal
- gone for good
- hidden
- look the other way

- pay no attention to me
- so distant, turn away
- stand far off, stand far away

c. Praise & Prayer Journal

1. What is *not* hidden from God? (Answers could include: my sighing, my guilt in days of trouble.)

2. What should we do when we need God's help but He seems hidden from us? (Among the answers: keep praying, confess our sins, examine ourselves.)

3. Who provides biblical examples of this characteristic, attribute, or action of God? (Answers could include: Joseph, Moses, David, Elijah.)

4. At times, do you feel as though God is hidden from you?

5. When has God hidden you and your family in His shelter, keeping you safe from the wicked?

47

HOLY: God is above all, extraordinary, mighty, lives in His sacred home/holy mountain, and sits on His holy throne. He is spiritually perfect, pure and sinless.

Ps. 3:4   "I call out to the LORD, and he answers me from his <u>holy</u> mountain."

Ps. 11:4   "The LORD is in his <u>holy</u> temple; the LORD is on his heavenly throne. He observes everyone on earth; his eyes examine them."

Ps. 22:3   "Yet you are enthroned as the <u>Holy</u> One; you are the one Israel praises."

Ps. 24:3   "Who may ascend the mountain of the LORD? Who may stand in his <u>holy</u> place?"

Ps. 28:2   "Hear my cry for mercy as I call to you for help, as I lift up my hands toward your Most <u>Holy</u> Place."

Ps. 29:2   "Ascribe to the LORD the glory due his name; worship the LORD in the splendor of his <u>holiness</u>."

Ps. 30:4   "Sing the praises of the LORD, you his faithful people; praise his <u>holy</u> name."

Ps. 33:21   "In him our hearts rejoice, for we trust in his <u>holy</u> name."

Ps. 46:4   "There is a river whose streams make glad the city of God, the <u>holy</u> place where the Most High dwells."

Ps. 47:8   "God reigns over the nations; God is seated on his <u>holy</u> throne."

Ps. 48:1   "Great is the LORD, and most worthy of praise, in the city of our God, his <u>holy</u> mountain."

Ps. 51:11   "Do not cast me from your presence or take your <u>Holy</u> Spirit from me."

Ps. 68:5   "A father to the fatherless, a defender of widows, is God in his <u>holy</u> dwelling."

Ps. 77:13   "Your ways, God, are <u>holy</u>. What god is as great as our God?"

Ps. 79:1   "O God, the nations have invaded your inheritance; they have defiled your holy temple, they have reduced Jerusalem to rubble."

Ps. 89:18   " . . . our king to the <u>Holy</u> One of Israel."

Ps. 89:35   "Once for all, I have sworn by my <u>holiness</u>—and I will not lie to David."

Ps. 93:5   "Your statutes, Lord, stand firm; <u>holiness</u> adorns your house for endless days."

Ps. 96:9   "Worship the Lord in the splendor of his <u>holiness</u>; tremble before him, all the earth."

Ps. 97:12   "Rejoice in the Lord, you who are righteous, and praise his <u>holy</u> name."

Ps. 98:1   "Sing to the Lord a new song, for he has done marvelous things; his right hand and his <u>holy</u> arm have worked salvation for him."

Ps. 99:3   "Let them praise your great and awesome name—he is <u>holy</u>."

Ps. 99:5   "Exalt the Lord our God and worship at his footstool; he is <u>holy</u>."

Ps. 99:9   "Exalt the Lord our God and worship at his <u>holy</u> mountain, for the Lord our God is <u>holy</u>."

Ps. 103:1   "Praise the Lord, my soul; all my inmost being, praise his <u>holy</u> name."

Ps. 105:3   "Glory in his <u>holy</u> name; let the hearts of those who seek the Lord rejoice."

Ps. 106:47   "Save us, Lord our God, and gather us from the nations, that we may give thanks to your <u>holy</u> name and glory in your praise."

Ps. 111:9   "He provided redemption for his people; he ordained his covenant forever— <u>holy</u> and awesome is his name."

Ps. 145:21   "My mouth will speak in praise of the Lord. Let every creature praise his <u>holy</u> name for ever and ever."

a. Hebrew/Strong's/biblical use

- holy thing
- sanctuary

b. Other versions/translations

- above it all
- extraordinary
- holiness

- mighty
- sacred home
- sanctuary

c. Praise & Prayer Journal

1. What are God's holy attributes? (Answers could include: His holy name, the Holy Spirit, the Holy One, His arm.)

2. Where are God's holy locations? (Answers could include: the temple, His throne, His place, His mountain, His dwelling, His sanctuary.)

3. What are biblical examples of this characteristic, attribute, or action of God? (Answers include: Abraham welcoming the three angels, Moses standing on holy ground, Moses not looking until God passed by, Isaiah's vision of God on His throne [Isaiah 6].)

4. Describe how you feel and sense God's holiness. (Answers include: in worship, in prayer, in church, in praise.)

48

HOPE: God wants us to put our hope in His unfailing love, His word, and His Lordship, including waiting, expecting, trusting, relying, and depending on Him in confidence.

Ps. 33:22   "May your unfailing love be with us, LORD, even as we put our <u>hope</u> in you."

Ps. 39:7   "But now, Lord, what do I look for? My <u>hope</u> is in you."

Ps. 43:5   "Put your <u>hope</u> in God, for I will yet praise him, my Savior and my God."

Ps. 69:6   "May those who <u>hope</u> in you not be disgraced because of me . . . "

Ps. 71:5   "For you have been my <u>hope</u>, Sovereign LORD, my confidence since my youth."

Ps. 119:114   "You are my refuge and my shield; I have put my <u>hope</u> in your word."

Ps. 146:5   "Blessed are those whose help is the God of Jacob, whose <u>hope</u> is in the LORD their God."

Ps. 147:11   "The LORD delights in those who fear him, who put their <u>hope</u> in his unfailing love."

a. Hebrew/Strong's/biblical use

- expectation, hope, live
- thing that I long for
- to look patiently, wait (for, on, upon)
- to wait, hope, expect, tarry, trust

b. Other versions/translations

- confidence
- depend
- keep me going

- look to you
- rely
- trust

c. Praise & Prayer Journal

1. How does one's hope in God strengthen a person's faith walk with God? (Answers could include: like Joseph's hope and faith; like Job; like Shadrach, Meshach, and Abednego [Daniel 3].)

2. What are other biblical examples of this characteristic, attribute, or action of God? (Answers could include: Daniel, Nehemiah, the prophets who endured persecution, the apostles enduring persecution to build the early church.)

3. How blessed are we that we can depend, rely, and trust that God will give us confidence to keep us going?

4. Describe a time you and your family put your hope in God.

49

HUMBLES: God can cause us and others to bend, kneel, bow down, and be subdued.

Ps. 18:39   "You armed me with strength for battle; you <u>humbled</u> my adversaries before me."

Ps. 44:9   "But now you have rejected and <u>humbled</u> us; you no longer go out with our armies."

Ps. 55:19   "God, who is enthroned from of old, who does not change—he will hear them and <u>humble</u> them, because they have no fear of God."

a. Hebrew/Strong's/biblical use

- to bend, kneel, bow, bow down
- to bend down, be humbled
- to cast away (off)
- to kneel in reverence
- to remove far away
- to sink down to one's knees

b. Other versions/translations

- affect
- brought us to dishonor
- deal with them
- disgraced
- embarrassed
- humiliate
- made to bow
- made us low
- make kneel
- put us to shame
- puts them in their place
- smashed
- subdued
- suffer

c. Praise & Prayer Journal

1. Who did God humble, and how: Joseph? (Answers could include: sold into slavery and thrown in jail.) Moses after killing the Egyptian? (Answers could include: exiled to a foreign land, made to tend sheep for forty years.) The Prodigal Son?

2. What are other biblical examples of this characteristic, attribute, or action of God? (Answers could include: Adam and Eve, Job, David, Solomon, Jonah.)

3. When has God humbled us and our families?

4. When has God humbled our adversaries and enemies?

5. How do we humble ourselves? (Answers could include: bending, kneeling, bowing down, approaching in reverence.)

50 **INSTRUCTS**: God advises, confirms, gives counsel, resolves, teaches, guides, gives good advice, warns.

Ps. 16:7   "I will praise the LORD, who counsels me; even at night my heart <u>instructs</u> me."

Ps. 25:8   "Good and upright is the LORD; therefore he <u>instructs</u> sinners in his ways."

Ps. 25:12   "He will <u>instruct</u> them in the ways they should choose."

Ps 32:8   "I will <u>instruct</u> you and teach you in the way you should go; I will counsel you with my loving eye on you."

a. Hebrew/Strong's/biblical use

- resolve, determine, purpose
- to advise, give counsel
- to instruct, teach

b. Other versions/translations

- confirms
- good advice
- guide
- reflect and learn

- sends, shows
- teaches
- warns

c. Praise & Prayer Journal

1. God instructs us in ways to choose and ways we should go. For sinners, His ways are to move someone to meet His goodness and uprightness. How have you seen God take these actions?

2. What are biblical examples of this characteristic, attribute, or action of God? (Answers could include: Noah, Moses, Solomon in building the great temple, Jonah, the prophets.)

3. How has God instructed you and your family?

4. When have you and your family felt God's instruction, confirmation, good advice, guidance, teachings, or warnings?

51 JUDGES: God does what is fair, straightens out, sets everything right, takes charge, and judges fairly in righteousness.

Ps. 7:11	"God is a righteous judge, a God who displays his wrath every day."
Ps. 9:4	"For you have upheld my right and my cause, sitting enthroned as the righteous judge."
Ps. 9:8	"He rules the world in righteousness and judges the peoples with equity."
Ps. 11:7	"For the LORD is righteous, he loves justice; the upright will see his face."
Ps. 18:20	"The LORD has dealt with me according to my righteousness."
Ps. 48:11	"Mount Zion rejoices . . . because of your judgments."
Ps. 50:4	"He summons the heavens above, and the earth, that he may judge his people."
Ps. 50:6	"And the heavens proclaim his righteousness, for he is a God of justice."

Ps. 75:7	"It is God who <u>judges</u> . . . "
Ps. 76:9	" . . . when you, God, rose up to <u>judge</u>, to save all the afflicted of the land."
Ps. 82:8	"Rise up, O God, <u>judge</u> the earth, for all the nations are your inheritance."
Ps. 94:2	"Rise up, <u>judge</u> of the earth; pay back to the proud what they deserve."
Ps. 96:10	"The world is firmly established, it cannot be moved; he will <u>judge</u> the peoples with equity."
Ps. 96:13	"Let all creation rejoice before the Lord, for he comes, he comes to <u>judge</u> the earth. He will judge the world in righteousness and the peoples in his faithfulness."
Ps. 98:9	"Let them sing before the Lord, for he comes to <u>judge</u> the earth. He will <u>judge</u> the world in righteousness and the peoples with equity."
Ps. 110:6	"He will <u>judge</u> the nations . . . "

a. Hebrew/Strong's/biblical use

- judgment, justice
- righteousness
- to contend, plead
- to judge

b. Other versions/translations

- do what is fair
- godly deeds
- judge fairly
- just decision; just legal decisions
- punish
- righteous way of life; righteous deeds
- solemn honor; set everything right
- straighten out
- taking charge; take people to court

c. Praise & Prayer Journal

1. Who does God judge? (Answers could include: His people, the peoples of the world, the nations, the entire earth.)

2. How does God judge? (Answers could include: with righteousness, with equity, for those who love justice.)

3. What are biblical examples of this characteristic, attribute, or action of God? (Answers include: the great flood, Sodom and Gomorrah, David's enemies, Esther exposing Haman's plot to destroy the Jews.)

4. Has God exhibited this action and attribute in your life? He may have done so by doing what is fair, straightening out, setting everything right, taking charge, judging fairly, and/or being righteous.

52 JUSTICE (JUST): God does what is fair, the right things are done in fairness, He treats fairly, He rules with equity, He secures justice.

Ps. 7:6   " . . . rise up against the rage of my enemies. Awake, my God; decree justice."

Ps. 9:8   "He rules the world in righteousness and judges the peoples with equity."

Ps. 9:16   "The LORD is known by his acts of justice . . . "

Ps. 11:7   "For the LORD is righteous, he loves justice; the upright will see his face."

Ps. 33:5   "The LORD loves righteousness and justice; the earth is full of his unfailing love."

Ps. 36:6   "Your righteousness is like the highest mountains, your justice like the great deep."

Ps. 50:6   "And the heavens proclaim his righteousness, for he is a God of justice."

Ps. 89:14 "Righteousness and justice are the foundation of your throne; love and faithfulness go before you."

Ps. 97:2   "Clouds and thick darkness surround him; righteousness and <u>justice</u> are the foundation of his throne."

Ps. 103:6   "The LORD works righteousness and <u>justice</u> for all the oppressed."

Ps. 140:12   "I know that the LORD secures <u>justice</u> for the poor and upholds the cause of the needy."

a. Hebrew/Strong's/biblical use

- judgment, justice
- righteousness

b. Other versions/translations

- do what is fair
- fairly, fairness, fair
- just, judgments
- pronounce judgment
- right thing done
- treated fairly
- uprightness

c. Praise & Prayer Journal

1. What other attribute appears mostly (combined with) the use of *justice*? (Answer: *righteousness*, used eight times in the Psalms list above.)

2. What are biblical examples of this characteristic, attribute, or action of God?

3. Who does the Lord secure justice for, upholding their cause? (Among the answers: the poor, the needy.)

4. Have you and your family experienced or seen God's justice?

53

KINDNESS: God gives us grace, does acts of loyal love, exhibits faithfulness, and His kindness is unfailing to His anointed.

Ps. 18:50   "He gives his king great victories; he shows unfailing <u>kindness</u> to his anointed, to David and to his descendants forever."

Ps. 36:7   "How precious is your <u>lovingkindness</u>, O God . . . "

Ps. 106:7   "When our ancestors were in Egypt, they gave no thought to your miracles; they did not remember your many <u>kindnesses</u>, and they rebelled by the sea, the Red Sea."

a. Hebrew/Strong's/biblical use

- covenant: keeping loyalty, faithfulness, kindness
- grace, lovingkindness

b. Other versions/translations

- acts of loyal love
- faithful
- great and wonderful love
- kindnesses, kind acts
- love
- mercy, mercies
- steadfast love

c. Praise & Prayer Journal:

1. How do you, personally, know God's kindness? (Answers could include: through his unfailing love, loyalty, mercy.)

2. What are biblical examples of this characteristic, attribute, or action of God?

3. Discuss/reflect on some ways God has been kind to your family.

54

KNOWS: God perceives, finds out, understands, keeps track of; we can't hide things from Him. God has infinite knowledge and is omniscient.

Ps. 44:21 " . . . would not God have discovered it, since he <u>knows</u> the secrets of the heart?"

Ps. 50:11 "I <u>know</u> every bird in the mountains, and the creatures in the fields are mine."

Ps. 69:5 "You, God, <u>know</u> my folly; my guilt is not hidden from you."

Ps. 69:19 "You <u>know</u> how I am scorned, disgraced, and shamed; all my enemies are before you."

Ps. 73:11 "They say, 'How would God <u>know</u>? Does the Most High <u>know</u> anything?'"

Ps. 94:11 "The Lord <u>knows</u> all human plans; he <u>knows</u> that they are futile."

Ps. 139:1 "You have searched me, Lord, and you <u>know</u> me."

Ps. 139:23 "Search me, God, and <u>know</u> my heart; test me and <u>know</u> my anxious thoughts."

Ps. 142:3 "When my spirit grows faint within me, it is you who <u>know</u> my way."

Ps. 147:5 "Great is our Lord and mighty in power, his understanding has no limit."

a. Hebrew/Strong's/biblical use

- finds out, discerns, understands
- perceives
- to know

b. Other versions/translations

- have knowledge
- keep track of
- knowest
- known
- we can't hide things from Him

c. Praise & Prayer Journal

1. What does God know? (Among numerous answers: all things, me, my heart, all secrets, every creature and every bird, our folly, all human plans, my anxious thoughts.)

2. What are biblical examples of this characteristic, attribute, or action of God? (Answers could include: God knew what Adam and Eve did, God knew of David's great sin, God knew the hearts of the many Judahite and Israelite kings [good and bad], God knew Nebuchadnezzar's dreams.)

3. How should we live and act since: (1) God keeps track of us; (2) we can't hide things from Him; (3) He is all-knowing; and (4) He is all-seeing?

55   LIFTS: God restores, rescues, straightens, raises up, and gives a fresh start.

Ps. 3:3   "But you, LORD, are a shield around me, my glory, the One who <u>lifts</u> my head high."

Ps. 9:13   "Have mercy and <u>lift</u> me up from the gates of death."

Ps. 10:12   "Arise, LORD! <u>Lift</u> up your hand, O God. Do not forget the helpless."

Ps. 46:6   "Nations are in uproar, kingdoms fall; he <u>lifts</u> his voice, the earth melts."

Ps. 113:7   "He raises the poor from the dust and <u>lifts</u> the needy from the ash heap."

Ps. 145:14   "The LORD upholds all who fall and <u>lifts</u> up all who are bowed down."

Ps. 146:8   "The LORD gives sight to the blind, the LORD <u>lifts</u> up those who are bowed down, the LORD loves the righteous."

a. Hebrew/Strong's/biblical use

- to lift, bear up—carry
- to lift, comfort—raise up
- to rise, be high

b. Other versions/translations

- gives a shout, gives a fresh start
- holds
- pulled me back, punish the wicked
- restores, raised, rescues, raises up
- snatch me away, snatch me back

- show your power
- speaks
- straightens
- strike him down
- take me away

c. Praise & Prayer Journal

1. Who does God lift? (Answers could include: those or all who are bowed down [two times in the Psalms list above], the needy, the brokenhearted.)

2. How does God lift us? (Answers could include: he lifts my head high, he lifts us up from death.)

3. When in the Bible did God lift His voice? (Answers include: Moses receiving the Ten Commandments, the baptism of Jesus, at the transfiguration of Jesus.)

4. What are other biblical examples of this characteristic, attribute, or action of God?

5. When has God lifted you and your family?

56 LIGHT/LIGHTS: God shines, enlightens, is glorious, looks with favor, and can light our path.

Ps. 13:3	"Look on me and answer, Lord my God. Give <u>light</u> to my eyes, or I will sleep in death."
Ps. 19:8	"The precepts of the Lord are right, giving joy to the heart. The commands of the Lord are radiant, giving <u>light</u> to the eyes."
Ps. 27:1	"The Lord is my <u>light</u> and my salvation . . . "
Ps. 36:9	"For with you is the fountain of life; in your <u>light</u> we see <u>light</u>."
Ps. 43:3	"Send me your <u>light</u> and your faithful care, let them lead me; let them bring me to your holy mountain, to the place where you dwell."

Ps. 44:3   "It was not by their sword that they won the land, nor did their arm bring them victory; it was your right hand, your arm, and the <u>light</u> of your face, for you loved them."

Ps. 50:2   "From Zion, perfect in beauty, God <u>shines</u> forth."

Ps. 76:4   "You are radiant with <u>light</u>, more majestic than mountains rich with game."

Ps. 89:15   "Blessed are those who have learned to acclaim you, who walk in the <u>light</u> of your presence, O LORD."

Ps. 90:8   "You have set our iniquities before you, our secret sins in the <u>light</u> of your presence."

Ps. 97:4   "His lightning <u>lights</u> up the world; the earth sees and trembles."

Ps. 104:2   "The LORD wraps himself in <u>light</u> as with a garment; he stretches out the heavens like a tent."

Ps. 118:27 "The LORD is God, and he has made his <u>light</u> shine on us."

Ps. 119:105 "Your word is a lamp for my feet, a <u>light</u> on my path."

Ps. 119:130 "The unfolding of your words gives <u>light</u>; it gives understanding to the simple."

Ps. 136:7   " . . . who made the great <u>lights</u> . . . "

a. Hebrew/Strong's/biblical use

- bright, light
- shine (forth)
- specifically: a chandelier

- to be or become light, shine, light
- to shine, be light, show self (cause to)

b. Other versions/translations

- blazes
- comes in splendor
- enlighten, easy
- flashes
- glorious
- insight

- lighten, lantern, lit up, light up
- looked on them with favor
- resplendent
- restore the sparkle
- shine, shone, shined, sunshine

c. Praise & Prayer Journal

1. What kind of light should we pray for? (Answers could include: a light on our path, a light to shine on us to give us understanding.)

2. How do you know God's light? (Answers could include: it shines forth, blazes, gives glorious insight, reveals His presence.)

3. Did Paul experience the light of Jesus on the road to Damascus? (Read Acts 9 for a full answer.)

4. What are other biblical examples of this characteristic, attribute, or action of God? (Answers could include: God's light that Moses saw when he received the Ten Commandments, Jesus shining forth His light in the transfiguration.)

57 LISTEN/LISTENS: God hears, bends an ear, pays attention, and responds.

Ps. 10:17   "You, LORD, hear the desire of the afflicted; you encourage them, and you <u>listen</u> to their cry."

Ps. 22:24   "For he has not despised or scorned the suffering of the afflicted one; he has not hidden his face from him but has <u>listened</u> to his cry for help."

Ps. 39:12   "Hear my prayer, LORD, <u>listen</u> to my cry for help."

Ps. 54:2   "Hear my prayer, O God; <u>listen</u> to the words of my mouth."

Ps. 61:1   "Hear my cry, O God; <u>listen</u> to my prayer."

Ps. 86:6   "Hear my prayer, LORD; <u>listen</u> to my cry for mercy."

Ps. 142:6   "<u>Listen</u> to my cry, for I am in desperate need; rescue me from those who pursue me, for they are too strong for me."

Ps. 143:1   "LORD, hear my prayer, <u>listen</u> to my cry for mercy; in your faithfulness and rightousness come to my relief."

a. Hebrew/Strong's/biblical use

- to broaden out the ear (with the hand)
- to hear, be attentive, heed
- to hear, listen, obey

b. Other versions/translations

- attend
- bend an ear
- cause thine ear to hear
- give ear, give heed
- heard, hear
- listening, listened
- open your ears
- pay close attention, pay attention
- responded

c. Praise & Prayer Journal

1. What does God listen for? (Answers include: our cry [two times from the Psalms list above], a cry for help, the words of our mouth, prayer, a cry for mercy [two times from the Psalms list above].)

2. Name some biblical examples of this characteristic, attribute, or action of God? (Answers include: Noah, Abraham, Jacob, Job, David, the prophets.)

3. Does this mean we can be verbal with our prayers? Is it OK to cry for help?

4. When was God attentive (paid attention) to your communication with Him?

58 **LOOKS (OBSERVES):** God watches everyone closely; He cares, watches, takes note; His eyes see, His eyes take everything in, He observes everyone on Earth; and He looks with kindness on the lowly.

Ps. 11:4   The LORD is in his holy temple; the LORD is on his heavenly throne. He <u>observes</u> everyone on earth; his eyes examine them."

Ps. 14:2   "The LORD <u>looks</u> down from heaven on all mankind to see if there are any who understand, any who seek God."

Ps. 33:13   "From heaven the LORD <u>looks</u> down and sees all mankind."

Ps. 53:2   "God <u>looks</u> down from heaven on all mankind to see if there is any who understand, any who seek God."

Ps. 85:11   "Faithfulness springs forth from the earth, and righteousness <u>looks</u> down from heaven."

Ps. 102:19 "The LORD <u>looked</u> down from his sanctuary on high."

Ps. 113:6   "The One who sits enthroned on high, who stoops down to <u>look</u>."

Ps. 138:6   "Though the LORD is exalted, he <u>looks</u> kindly on the lowly; though lofty, he sees them from afar."

a. Hebrew/Strong's/biblical use

- eyes beheld
- eyes taking everything in
- observes
- overhang, look out and down
- sees
- to look, regard
- to overlook, look down or out (as out of a window)
- to see, look at
- watches

b. Other versions/translations

- cares
- His eyes behold
- His eyes see
- His eyes take everything in
- regards, respect
- sticks head out of, sees
- takes note
- watches
- watches everyone closely

c. Praise & Prayer Journal

1. What does God actively do? (Answers could include: look down [used five times in the Psalms list above], stoops down to look.)

2. Who does the LORD look for, or at, or observe? (Answers could include: everyone, all

mankind [used two times in the Psalms list above], those who understand and seek God, and kindly on the lowly.)

3. What are biblical examples of this characteristic, attribute, or action of God? (Answers could include: the righteousness of Noah and his family; God's people in slavery while in Egypt; Rachel, Hannah, and other women who could not bear children.)

4. When have you and your family been thankful God was looking at your situation?

59 LOVES: God's love is unfailing, endures forever, and is full of grace, compassion, goodness, mercy, rewards, kindness. He is ready to forgive.

Ps. 6:4	"Turn, Lord, and deliver me; save me because of your unfailing <u>love</u>."
Ps. 11:7	"For the Lord is righteous, he <u>loves</u> justice; the upright will see his face."
Ps. 13:5	"But I trust in your unfailing <u>love</u> . . . "
Ps. 17:7	"Show the wonder of your great <u>love</u> . . . "
Ps. 23:6	"Surely your goodness and <u>love</u> will follow me all the days of my life, and I will dwell in the house of the Lord forever."
Ps. 25:6	"Remember, Lord, your great mercy and <u>love</u>, for they are from of old."
Ps. 25:7	"Do not remember the sins of my youth and my rebellious ways; according to your <u>love</u> remember me, for you, Lord, are good."
Ps. 25:10	"All the ways of the Lord are <u>loving</u> and faithful . . . "
Ps. 31:16	"Let your face shine on your servant; save me in your unfailing <u>love</u>."
Ps. 31:21	"Praise be to the Lord, for He showed his wonderful <u>love</u> to me."

Ps. 32:10   " . . . but the LORD's unfailing <u>love</u> surrounds the one who trusts in him."

Ps. 33:5   "The LORD <u>loves</u> righteousness and justice; the earth is full of His unfailing <u>love</u>."

Ps. 33:18   "But the eyes of the LORD are on those who fear him, on those whose hope is in his unfailing <u>love</u>."

Ps. 33:22   "May your unfailing <u>love</u> be with us, LORD, even as we put our hope in you."

Ps. 36:5   "Your <u>love</u>, LORD, reaches to the heavens, your faithfulness to the skies."

Ps. 36:7   "How priceless is your unfailing <u>love</u>, O God!"

Ps. 36:10   "Continue your <u>love</u> to those who know you . . . "

Ps. 37:28   "For the LORD <u>loves</u> the just . . . "

Ps. 40:11   " . . . may your <u>love</u> and faithfulness always protect me."

Ps. 42:8   "By day the LORD directs his <u>love</u>, at night his song is with me—a prayer to the God of my life."

Ps. 44:3   " . . . and the light of your face, for you <u>loved</u> them."

Ps. 44:26   "Rise up and help us; rescue us because of your unfailing <u>love</u>."

Ps. 45:7   "You <u>love</u> righteousness and hate wickedness . . . "

Ps. 48:9   "Within your temple, O God, we meditate on your unfailing <u>love</u>."

Ps. 51:1   "Have mercy upon me, O God, according to your unfailing <u>love</u>, according to your great compassion blot out my transgressions."

Ps. 52:8   "I trust in God's unfailing <u>love</u> for ever and ever."

Ps. 57:3   "God sends his <u>love</u> and his faithfulness."

Ps. 57:10   "For great is your <u>love</u>, reaching to the heavens; your faithfulness reaches to the skies."

Ps. 62:11   " . . . and that you, O LORD, are <u>loving</u>."

Ps. 62:12   " . . . and with you, LORD, is unfailing <u>love</u>."

Ps. 63:3   "Because your <u>love</u> is better than life . . . "

Ps. 69:16   "Answer me, LORD, out of the goodness of your <u>love</u>; in your great mercy turn to me."

Ps. 85:7   "Show us your unfailing <u>love</u>, LORD, and grant us your salvation."

Ps. 86:5   "You, LORD, are forgiving and good, abounding in <u>love</u> to all who call to you."

Ps. 88:11   "Is your <u>love</u> declared in the grave . . . ?"

Ps. 89:1   "I will sing of the LORD's great <u>love</u> forever."

Ps. 89:2   "I will declare that your <u>love</u> stands firm forever."

Ps. 89:14   " . . . <u>love</u> and faithfulness go before you."

Ps. 89:24   "My faithful <u>love</u> will be with him . . . "

Ps. 89:49   "LORD, where is your former great <u>love</u>, which in your faithfulness you swore to David?"

Ps. 90:14   "Satisfy us in the morning with your unfailing <u>love</u>, that we may sing for joy and be glad all our days."

Ps. 92:2   " . . . proclaiming your <u>love</u> in the morning and your faithfulness at night."

Ps. 94:18   "Your unfailing <u>love</u>, LORD, supported me."

Ps. 99:4   "The King is mighty, he <u>loves</u> justice—you have established equity."

Ps. 103:8   "The LORD is compassionate and gracious, slow to anger, abounding in <u>love</u>."

Ps. 103:11   " . . . so great is his <u>love</u> for those who fear him."

Ps. 106:1   "Praise the LORD. Give thanks to the LORD, for he is good; his <u>love</u> endures forever."

Ps. 107:1   "Give thanks to the LORD, for he is good; his <u>love</u> endures forever."

Ps. 107:8   "Let them give thanks to the LORD for his unfailing <u>love</u> and his wonderful deeds for mankind."

Ps. 117:2   "For great is his <u>love</u> towards us . . . "

Ps. 118:4   "Let those who fear the LORD say: 'His <u>love</u> endures forever.'"

Ps. 119:64   "The earth is filled with your <u>love</u>, LORD; teach me your decrees."

Ps. 136:1   "Give thinks to the LORD, for he is good. His <u>love</u> endures forever."

Ps. 145:8   "The LORD is gracious and compassionate, slow to anger and rich in <u>love</u>."

Ps. 146:8   "…the LORD gives sight to the blind, the LORD lifts up those who are bowed down, the LORD <u>loves</u> the righteous."

a. Hebrew/Strong's/biblical use

- covenant—keeping loyalty, faithfulness, kindness
- grace, lovingkindness
- to be pleased with, be favorable to
- to love

b. Other versions/translations

- compassion
- delighted
- faithfulness, favored, faith deeds
- goodness
- lovingkindness

- mercy
- promotes, pleased, partial
- ready to forgive
- rewards

c. Praise & Prayer Journal

1. How do the Psalms describe God's love? (Answers include: as unfailing [used sixteen times in the Psalms list above], enduring forever [used seven times in the Psalms list above], abounding, out of His goodness, great, rich.)

2. What does God love? (Answers include: justice, being just, righteousness.)

3. What are biblical examples of this characteristic, attribute, or action of God? (Answers include: as shown to God's chosen race, Israel; to David; to the righteous.)

4. When have you and your family received God's unfailing and enduring love?

60

MAJESTIC: God's name, voice, and deeds are majestic; He is robed in splendor, honor, glory. He is powerful, excellent, magnificent, and great.

Ps. 8:1	"Lord, our Lord, how <u>majestic</u> is your name in all the earth! You have set your glory in the heavens."
Ps. 29:4	"The voice of the Lord is powerful; the voice of the Lord is <u>majestic</u>."
Ps. 76:4	"You are radiant with light, more <u>majestic</u> than mountains rich with game."
Ps. 93:1	"The Lord reigns, he is robed in <u>majesty</u>; the Lord is robed in <u>majesty</u> and armed with strength indeed; the world is established, firm and secure."
Ps. 111:3	"Glorious and <u>majestic</u> are his deeds, and his righteousness endures forever."

a. Hebrew/Strong's/biblical use

- excellent things, lifting up, majesty, pride, proudly
- great, majestic, powerful
- ornament, splendor, honor, majesty, glory
- splendor, majesty, vigor

b. Other versions/translations

- excellent
- honorable
- magnificent, majesty
- ruling
- strength

c. Praise & Prayer Journal

1. What is majestic? (Answers include: The Lord's name, His voice, He is robed in glory and majesty, His deeds.)

2. How majestic is God? (Answers include: more than the mountains, more than mountains rich with game, far more than any earthly king, more than our minds can conceive.)

3. What are biblical examples of this characteristic, attribute, or action of God? (Answers include: God in the temple; Job heard a voice roar and thunder, and then His majestic voice; Daniel and Ezekiel's visions; Jesus on the Mount of Transfiguration.)

4. How do you recognize God's majesty in your praises, prayers, and worship?

61

MAKES: God leads, guides, examines, defends, directs us, gives, provides, causes, removes obstacles, and provides safety, security, perfect ways, and firm steps.

Ps. 4:8	"Lord, <u>make</u> me dwell in safety."
Ps. 5:8	"... <u>make</u> your way straight before me."
Ps. 7:9	"Bring to an end the violence of the wicked and <u>make</u> the righteous secure."
Ps. 16:11	"You <u>make</u> known to me the path of life."
Ps. 18:32	"It is God who ... <u>makes</u> my way perfect."
Ps. 23:2	"He <u>makes</u> me lie down in green pastures, he leads me beside quiet waters."
Ps. 25:14	"The Lord confides in those who fear him; he <u>makes</u> his covenant known to them."
Ps. 37:6	"He will <u>make</u> your righteous reward shine like the dawn."
Ps. 37:23	"The Lord <u>makes</u> firm the steps of the one who delights in him."
Ps. 48:8	"As we have heard, so we have seen in the city of the Lord Almighty, in the city of our God: God <u>makes</u> her secure forever."
Ps. 67:1	"May God be gracious to us and bless us and <u>make</u> his face shine on us."
Ps. 80:7	"Restore us, God Almighty; <u>make</u> your face shine on us, that we may be saved."
Ps. 100:3	"Know that the Lord is God. It is he who <u>made</u> us and we are His."

Ps. 104:3   "He <u>makes</u> the clouds his chariot and rides on the wings of the wind."

Ps. 104:4   "He <u>makes</u> winds his messengers, flames of fire his servants."

Ps. 104:10   "He <u>makes</u> springs pour water into the ravines; it flows between the mountains."

Ps. 104:14   "He <u>makes</u> grass grow for the cattle, and plants for people to cultivate—bringing forth food from the earth."

Ps. 119:98   "Your commands are always with me and <u>make</u> me wiser than my enemies."

Ps. 119:135 "<u>Make</u> your face shine on your servant and teach me your decrees."

Ps. 135:7   "He <u>makes</u> clouds rise from the ends of the earth; he sends lightning with the rain and brings out the wind from his storehouses."

Ps. 147:8   "He covers the sky with clouds; he supplies the earth with rain and <u>makes</u> grass grow on the hills."

a. Hebrew/Strong's/biblical use

- to be established, prepared
- to do, make, accomplish, fashion
- to examine, try, prove
- to give, put, make
- to impose timbers (for roof or floor), make beams to floor
- to lead, guide (by implication, to transport)
- to send, send away
- to sprout, spring up, grow up
- to stretch one's self out, lie stretched out, make to rest

b. Other versions/translations

- aimed
- bring forth
- causes, commanded
- defend, directs, directed
- establish
- let, lays
- made
- provides
- remove the obstacles
- show, started, sends
- tests, tries, turn
- to send, send away
- to sprout, spring up, grow up

c. Praise & Prayer Journal

1. What does God make for us or do for us? (Answers could include: safety, security, perfects our ways, firm steps, wiser, grass grow, pours out water.)

2. How does God make His light shine on us, and what are biblical examples of this? (Answers could include: Abraham, Joseph, Moses and the Ten Commandments.)

3. What are biblical examples of this characteristic, attribute, or action of God? (Answers include: God's Creation, days one to six; Abraham's journeys; God made a way for Joseph to be a leader in Egypt and later saved the Israelites from famine; God directed the Israelites out of Egypt; God parted the Red Sea and the Jordan River; He made water come out of a rock for Moses; leading Joshua.)

4. When has God shined on you and your family His blessings? When has He provided safety, security, and firm steps? When has He removed obstacles?

62   MERCIFUL: God is compassionate, gracious, kindly, shows me favor, and is full of lovingkindness.

Ps. 4:1   "Give me relief from my distress; have <u>mercy</u> on me and hear my prayer."

Ps. 6:2   "Have <u>mercy</u> on me, LORD, for I am faint; heal me, LORD, for my bones are in agony."

Ps. 9:13   "LORD, see how my enemies persecute me! Have <u>mercy</u> and lift me up from the gates of death."

Ps. 25:7   "Remember not the sins of my youth, nor my transgression: according to thy <u>mercy</u>, remember thou me for thy goodness's sake, O LORD."

Ps. 25:10 "All the paths of the LORD are <u>mercy</u> and truth unto such as keep his covenant and his testimonies."

Ps. 27:7   "Hear my voice when I call, LORD; be <u>merciful</u> to me and answer me."

Ps. 28:2   "Hear my cry for <u>mercy</u> as I call to you for help, as I lift up my hands toward your Most Holy Place."

Ps. 28:6   "Praise be to the LORD, for he has heard my cry for <u>mercy</u>."

Ps. 40:11   "Do not withhold your <u>mercy</u> from me, LORD."

Ps. 41:4   "I said, 'Have <u>mercy</u> on me, LORD; heal me, for I have sinned against you.'"

Ps. 41:10   "But may you have <u>mercy</u> on me, LORD; raise me up, that I may repay them."

Ps. 51:1   "Have <u>mercy</u> on me, O God, according to your unfailing love; according to your great compassion blot out my transgressions."

Ps. 57:1   "Have <u>mercy</u> on me, my God; have mercy on me, for in you I take refuge. I will take refuge in the shadow of your wings until the disaster has passed."

Ps. 69:16   "Answer me, LORD, out of the goodness of your love; in your great <u>mercy</u> turn to me."

Ps. 77:9   "Has God forgotten to be <u>merciful</u>? Has he in anger withheld his compassion?"

Ps. 78:38   "Yet he was <u>merciful</u>; he forgave their iniquities and did not destroy them. Time after time he restrained his anger and did not stir up his full wrath."

Ps. 79:8   "Do not hold against us the sins of past generations; may your <u>mercy</u> come quickly to meet us, for we are in desperate need."

Ps. 119:132 "Turn to me and have <u>mercy</u> on me, as you always do to those who love your name."

Ps. 123:3   "Have <u>mercy</u> on us, LORD, have <u>mercy</u> on us, for we have endured no end of contempt."

Ps. 143:1   "LORD, hear my prayer, listen to my cry for <u>mercy</u>; in your faithfulness and righteousness come to my relief."

a. Hebrew/Strong's/biblical use

- compassionate—full of compassion, merciful
- covenant—keeping loyalty, faithfulness, kindness, grace, lovingkindness

- to be gracious, pity
- to entreat

b. Other versions/translations

- compassion, compassionate
- gracious, give grace
- help
- kind, kindly
- love, lovingkindness
- mercy

- pity
- show me favor, faithful; full of tender love
- steadfast love, supplications
- unlimited compassion

c. Praise & Prayer Journal

1. The psalmists ask for: "mercy for me" (twelve times in the Psalms), "mercy for us" (two times in the Psalms), to hear my cry for mercy (three times in the Psalms). How might this affect your crying out to God?

2. Under what circumstances did those in the Bible ask for God's mercy? (Answers include: from those under distress, those who are faint, "for us," "for me," for those under persecution.)

3. What are biblical examples of this characteristic, attribute, or action of God? (Answers include: Adam and Eve, Abraham and Sarah, Joseph, the angel of death in Egypt passing over the doorposts of the Israelites that were covered with the blood of a sacrificed lamb, that He be merciful on the Israelites despite their making and worshipping a golden calf, David and his sin with Bathsheba.)

4. When has God been merciful or given relief from distress to you and your family?

63

MIGHTY: God is awesome, great, powerful, strong, including mightiness, gloriousness, greatness, and strength. He is omnipotent, having unlimited power and authority.

Ps. 24:8	"Who is this King of glory? The LORD strong and <u>mighty</u>, the LORD <u>mighty</u> in battle."
Ps. 50:1	"The <u>Mighty</u> One, God, the LORD, speaks and summons the earth."
Ps. 62:7	"My salvation and my honor depend on God; he is my <u>mighty</u> rock, my refuge."
Ps. 77:12	"I will consider all your works and meditate on all your <u>mighty</u> deeds."
Ps. 89:8	"Who is like you, LORD God Almighty? You, LORD, are <u>mighty</u>, and your faithfulness surrounds you."
Ps. 89:9	"O LORD God Almighty, who is like you, you are <u>mighty</u> . . . "
Ps. 89:13	"Your arm is endowed with power; your hand is <u>strong</u>, your right hand exalted."
Ps. 89:17	"For you are their glory and <u>strength</u> . . . "
Ps. 93:4	"<u>Mightier</u> than the thunder of the great waters, <u>mightier</u> than the breakers of the sea—the LORD on high is <u>mighty</u>."
Ps. 118:15	"Shouts of joy and victory resound in the tents of the righteous: 'The LORD's right hand has done <u>mighty</u> things!'"
Ps. 118:16	"The LORD's right hand is lifted high; the LORD's right hand has done <u>mighty</u> things!"
Ps. 145:4	"One generation commends your works to another; they tell of your <u>mighty</u> acts."
Ps. 145:12	" . . . so that all people may know of your <u>mighty</u> acts and the glorious splendor of your kingdom."
Ps. 147:5	"Great is our LORD and <u>mighty</u> in power; his understanding has no limit."

Ps. 150:1   "Praise the LORD. Praise God in his sanctuary; praise him in his mighty heavens."

a. Hebrew/Strong's/biblical use

- mighty, strong
- properly, firm, strong
- strength and security
- strength, might, wealth, army
- to be stout, harden, prevail, strength (self), be strong

b. Other versions/translations

- abundant, awesome
- glorious, great
- powerful
- strength, strong
- valiantly

c. Praise & Prayer Journal

1. How does God show His mightiness? (Answers could include: in His acts, power, heavens, things, deeds, and in battle.)

2. In the Bible, what mighty acts and deeds did God do? (Answers could include: created the heavens and the Earth, the great flood, provided a rainbow after the great flood, the plagues in Egypt, parting of the Red Sea, the walls falling in Jericho, the destruction of Israel's enemies.)

3. What are other biblical examples of this characteristic, attribute, or action of God?

64

MIRACLES: God does awesome and amazing feats, marvelous and wonderful things, including great wonders and wondrous works.

Ps. 77:11   "I will remember the deeds of the LORD; yes, I will remember your <u>miracles</u> of long ago."

Ps. 77:14   "You are the God who performs <u>miracles</u>; you display your power among the peoples."

Ps. 78:12   "He did <u>miracles</u> in the sight of their ancestors in the land of Egypt, in the region of Zoan."

Ps. 105:5   "Remember the wonders he has done, his <u>miracles</u>, and the judgments he pronounced."

Ps. 106:7   "They gave no thought to your <u>miracles</u>; they did not remember your many kindnesses."

Ps. 106:22   " . . . <u>miracles</u> in the land of Ham and awesome deeds by the Red Sea."

a. Hebrew/Strong's/biblical use

- a miracle: marvelous thing, wonder, wonderful, wonderfully
- sign, portent

b. Other versions/translations

- amazing things, amazing feats
- great wonders
- marvelous things
- miraculous deeds
- wonderful things, world of wonders
- wonders
- wonders, wondrous works

c. Praise & Prayer Journal

1. What are some of the miracles God performed in the Bible? (Answers include: God's miracles in Moses' dealing with Pharoah, the angel of death passing over Jewish homes that had the blood of a lamb over the doorposts, the parting of the Red Sea and Jordan River, Joshua and other leaders in their battles, manna from Heaven, the fallen walls of Jericho, Samson's final defeat of the Philistines.)

2. How are miracles often, or commonly, described? (Answers could include: as marvelous things, wonderful works, amazing things.)

3. What are other biblical examples of this characteristic, attribute, or action of God?

4. What miracles or awesome deeds has God done for you and your family?

65

PEACEGIVER: God gives safety, security, and promises; He blesses His people with peace.

Ps. 29:11   "The Lord gives strength to his people; the Lord blesses his people with <u>peace</u>."

Ps. 85:8   "I will listen to what God the Lord says; he promises <u>peace</u> to his people, his faithful servants—but let them not turn to folly."

Ps. 147:14   "He grants <u>peace</u> to your borders and satisfies you with the finest of wheat."

a. Hebrew/Strong's/biblical use

- completeness
- peace
- soundness

b. Other versions/translations

- safe and secure
- security

c. Praise & Prayer Journal

1. What kinds of peace does God give? (Answers could include: safety in our borders, safety in our households, the finest food and provisions, safety, security.)

2. God promises peace to whom? (Answers include: to His people.)

3. What are biblical examples of this characteristic, attribute, or action of God? (Answers could include: Abraham in his travels, the Israelites while wandering for forty years, Nehemiah rebuilding the walls and the peace provided by some of the neighbors during that rebuilding.)

4. When have you and your family overlooked God's working and failed to thank Him when He has given you peace, security, safeness, completeness, soundness?

66

PERFECT (PERFECTOR): God's way, and law, is whole, complete, perfection, straight, and smooth; and He gives right direction.

Ps. 18:30	"As for God, his way is <u>perfect</u>: The LORD's word is flawless; he shields all who take refuge in him."
Ps. 18:32	"It is God who . . . makes my way <u>perfect</u>."
Ps. 19:7	"The law of the LORD is <u>perfect</u>, refreshing the soul. The statutes of the LORD are trustworthy, making wise the simple."
Ps. 50:2	"From Zion, <u>perfect</u> in beauty, God shines forth."

a. Hebrew/Strong's/biblical use

- complete, whole
- perfection of beauty

b. Other versions/translations

- blameless
- faithful manner
- perfection
- removes obstacles in my way
- right direction
- straight and smooth
- whole

c. Praise & Prayer Journal

1. What are some of the things, or outcomes, that emanate from God and are perfect? (Answers could include: His way, His law, His right direction.)

2. What are biblical examples of this characteristic, attribute, or action of God? (Answers include: all creation, seen and unseen; in the Garden of Eden; Noah building the Ark; changing Pharaoh's heart so the Israelites could go free; the parting of the Red Sea.)

3. How is God the perfector? (Answers include: By removing obstacles in the way, making things straight and smooth and in the right direction, taking sinners and making them whole again.)

4. When has God's way been perfect in your life and your family's life?

67

PRESENT: God is always there, ready to help, takes the side of the person who trusts Him, and is available. God is omnipresent.

Ps. 14:5   "But there they are, overwhelmed with dread, for God is <u>present</u> in the company of the righteous."

Ps. 46:1   "God is our refuge and strength, an ever-<u>present</u> help in trouble."

Ps. 139:7   "Where can I go from your spirit? Where can I flee from your <u>presence</u>?"

a. Hebrew/Strong's/biblical use

- always there

b. Other versions/translations

- among those, always there
- ready to help
- takes the side of

- very present
- with

c. Praise & Prayer Journal

1. In what kind of company is God present? (Answers could include: the righteous, those who cry out to Him.)

2. What are biblical examples of this characteristic, attribute, or action of God? (Answers include: God with Abraham, Moses, and Joshua; God's pillars of clouds and pillars of fire while the Israelites were leaving Egypt; God's cloud resting above the tent of the tabernacle; God's cloud moving in the direction the Israelites were to go.)

3. In what circumstances is God present? (Answers include: when one who trusts Him is in trouble, when they are overwhelmed or in dread.)

4. When have you been thankful that God was present in your life or family circumstances and events?

68

PRESERVES: God is actively watching, guarding, saving, reviving, caring, protecting, watching over, and taking care of us.

Ps. 31:23　"The LORD <u>preserves</u> those who are true to him, but the proud he pays back in full."

Ps. 36:6　"O LORD, you <u>preserve</u> both man and beast."

Ps. 41:2　"The LORD protects and <u>preserves</u> them . . . "

Ps. 119:25　"I am laid low in the dust; <u>preserve</u> my life according to your word."

Ps. 119:37　"Turn my eyes away from worthless things; <u>preserve</u> my life according to your word."

Ps. 119:40　"How I long for your precepts! In your righteousness <u>preserve</u> my life."

Ps. 119:50　"Your promise <u>preserves</u> my life."

Ps. 119:88　"In your unfailing love <u>preserve</u> my life, that I may obey the statutes of your mouth."

Ps. 119:107　"I have suffered much; <u>preserve</u> my life, LORD, according to your word."

Ps. 119:149　"Hear my voice in accordance with your love; <u>preserve</u> my life, LORD, acording to your laws."

Ps. 119:154　"Defend my cause and redeem me; <u>preserve</u> my life according to your promise."

Ps. 119:156　"Your compassion, LORD, is great; <u>preserve</u> my life according to your laws."

Ps. 119:159　" . . . I love your precepts; <u>preserve</u> my life, LORD, in accordance with your love."

Ps. 138:7　"Though I walk in the midst of trouble, you <u>preserve</u> my life. You stretch out your hand against the anger of my foes; with your right hand you save me."

Ps. 143:11　"For your name's sake, LORD, <u>preserve</u> my life; in your rightousness, bring me out of trouble."

a. Hebrew/Strong's/biblical use

- to keep, guard, or serve
- to live, revive
- to save
- to watch, guard, keep

b. Other versions/translations

- cares for
- gives new life, gives me back
- keeps me alive
- protects
- puts me together again

- quickens me
- revives
- saves, spares my life
- takes care of
- watches over

c. Praise & Prayer Journal

1. What does God preserve? (Answers include: my life [used twelve times in the Psalms], man, beasts.)

2. How does God preserve? (Answers include: He watches, keeps, serves, guards, saves, revives, cares for, protects; He gives new life according to His love, His word, His promise, and His laws.)

3. What are biblical examples of this characteristic, attribute, or action of God? (Answers include: post-flood restoration; watching over the Israelites while departing from Egypt; David while being pursued by Saul; Job; Shadrach, Meshach, and Abednego in the fiery furnace; Jonah in the belly of the big fish.)

4. When has God preserved you and your family? Have you expressed your gratitude?

69 **PROMISES**: God takes charge, is commanding, and stays true to His instructions, His covenant, and His word.

Ps. 105:8   "He remembers his covenant forever, the <u>promise</u> he made, for a thousand generations."

Ps. 105:42   "For he remembered his holy <u>promise</u> given to his servant Abraham."

Ps. 106:12   "They believed His <u>promises</u> and sang His praise."

Ps. 119:38   "Fulfill your <u>promise</u> to your servant, so that you may be feared."

Ps. 119:41   "May your unfailing love come to me, Lᴏʀᴅ, your salvation, according to your <u>promise</u>."

Ps. 119:50   "My comfort in my suffering is this: your <u>promise</u> preserves my life."

Ps. 119:58   "I have sought your face with all my heart; be gracious to me according to your <u>promise</u>."

Ps. 119:76   "May your unfailing love be my comfort, according to your <u>promise</u> to your servant."

Ps. 119:116 "Sustain me, my God, according to your <u>promise</u>, and I will live; do not let my hopes be dashed."

Ps. 119:154 "Defend my cause and redeem me; preserve my life according to your <u>promise</u>."

Ps. 119:162 "I rejoice in your <u>promise</u> like one who finds great spoil."

Ps. 119:170 "May my supplication come before you; deliver me according to your <u>promise</u>."

a. Hebrew/Strong's/biblical use

- commandment, speech, word
- holy thing, sanctuary
- to command, charge
- word, thing, saying

b. Other versions/translations

- covenant
- instructions
- word he commanded
- word, what he said

c. Praise & Prayer Journal

1. What things are according to His promises? (Answers include: His covenants, instructions, the words He commanded and said, His preserving my life [used two times in the Psalms].)

2. What are other words used for promises? (Answers include: commands, charges, holy thing, word, saying.)

3. What are biblical examples of God's promises? (Answers could include: His covenant with Abraham, the Ten Commandments, His covenants with the Israelites, God's inspired words in all of the Bible.)

4. What are other biblical examples of this characteristic, attribute, or action of God? (Answers could include: God's promises to the Israelites of a land flowing with milk and honey; Joshua and the Israelite army walking seven times around the walls of Jericho, which then fell; Nehemiah's rebuilding of the walls, and his completion of that job.)

5. When have God's promises come true in your life and in the lives of your family?

70

PROTECTS: God helps, guards, watches, defends, keeps us safe, looks after us, preserves, rescues, stands guard around, shields, and takes care of us.

Ps. 12:5   "'I will now arise,'" says the LORD. "'I will <u>protect</u> them from those who malign them.'"

Ps. 12:7   "O LORD, you will keep us safe and <u>protect</u> us from such people forever."

Ps. 16:5   "You have made my lot secure."

Ps. 20:1   " . . . may the name of the God of Jacob <u>protect</u> you."

Ps. 32:7   "You are my hiding place; you will <u>protect</u> me from trouble and surround me with songs of deliverance."

Ps. 34:7   "The angel of the LORD encamps around those who fear him."

Ps. 34:20   " . . . He <u>protects</u> all his bones."

Ps. 37:28   "They will be <u>protected</u> forever . . ."

Ps. 40:11   "…may your love and your truth always <u>protect</u> me."

Ps. 41:2   "The LORD will <u>protect</u> him and preserve his life."

Ps. 69:29   "I am in pain and distress; may your salvation, O God, <u>protect</u> me."

Ps. 91:14   "'Because he loves me,' says the LORD, 'I will <u>protect</u> him, for he acknowledges my name.'"

Ps. 116:6   "The LORD <u>protects</u> the unwary; when I was brought low, he saved me."

Ps. 121:7   "The LORD will keep you from all harm."

Ps. 140:1   "Rescue me, LORD, from evildoers; <u>protect</u> me from the violent."

Ps. 140:4   "Keep me safe, LORD, from the hands of the wicked; <u>protect</u> me from the violent, who devise ways to trip my feet."

a. Hebrew/Strong's/biblical use

- deliverance, salvation, rescue, safety, welfare
- to bend down, encamp
- to help, follow close, maintain, retain, stay (up)
- to keep, guard, observe
- to watch, to guard (in a good sense), to keep

b. Other versions/translations

- best care
- continually shelter; circle of protection
- defend
- encamps
- guard
- keep you safe, keeps danger far from
- kept safe, keeps together
- looks after us
- maintain
- out of harm's way
- permanently secure
- place in safety; protect them
- provide the safety, preserves
- rescue
- set in safety; support
- shielding
- stands guard around; set on high
- watches over
- takes care of

c. Praise & Prayer Journal

1. God protects whom? (Answers include: us, you, me, the unwary, those who fear God; the angel of the LORD encamps around those who fear Him.)

2. God protects from what? (Answers include: from trouble, from the violent, from those who malign.)

3. What are useful translations of *to protect*? (Answers include: circle of protection, continually shelter, kept safe, best care, looks after us, out of harm's way, rescues, shielding, watches over, takes care of.)

4. What are biblical examples of this characteristic, attribute, or action of God? (Answers include: protecting Noah when he built the Ark, protecting the Israelites leaving Egypt, protecting David and Joshua in their battles, protecting Nehemiah when the Israelites were rebuilding the walls.)

5. When has God protected you and your family? Your home? Your travel? Your work?

71 PROVIDES: God provides by giving, delivering, enlarging, making us lack no good thing, giving everything we need.

Ps. 18:28	"You, O LORD, keep my lamp burning . . . "
Ps. 18:36	"You <u>provide</u> a broad path for my feet, so that my ankles do not give way."
Ps. 22:26	"The poor will eat and be satisfied . . . "
Ps. 34:9	" . . . for those who fear him lack nothing."
Ps. 34:10	" . . . those who seek the LORD lack no good thing."
Ps. 65:9	"The streams of God are filled with water to <u>provide</u> the people with grain, for so you have ordained it."
Ps. 68:9	"You gave abundant shower, O God."
Ps. 68:10	" . . . You <u>provided</u> for the poor."
Ps. 104:27	"All look to you to give them their food at the proper time."
Ps. 105:24	"The LORD made his people very fruitful."
Ps. 111:5	"He <u>provides</u> food for those who fear him."

Ps. 111:9   "He <u>provided</u> redemption for his people; he ordained his covenant forever—holy and awesome is his name."

Ps. 147:9   "He <u>provides</u> food for the cattle and for the young ravens when they call."

a. Hebrew/Strong's/biblical use

- to be established, prepared
- to be or grow wide, be or grow large
- to give, put, make
- to send, send away

b. Other versions/translations

- caused
- delivered
- enlarged
- gave
- have everything they need
- lack nothing; lack no good thing
- made
- never in need; not be in want of any good thing
- prepare
- sent
- there is no want
- will have all they need

c. Praise & Prayer Journal

1. For who or what does God provide? (Answers include: redemption, a broad path for our feet, for His people, for the poor, for the needy, food; for cattle, young ravens, all beasts of the field; and for those who fear Him.)

2. What are other translations of *to provide*? (Answers include: to grow large, to give, delivered, enlarged, lack nothing, lack no good thing.)

3. What are additional biblical examples of this characteristic, attribute, or action of God? (Answers could include: manna and water for the Israelites in the desert, food for the prophet Elijah during famine.)

4. Name some of the many things God has provided for you and your family.

72

PUNISHES: God disciplines, corrects, takes vengeance, and takes revenge, including leveling His wrath, anger, and judgment.

Ps. 11:6   "On the wicked he will rain fiery coals and burning sulfur."

Ps. 38:3   "Because of your <u>wrath</u> there is no health in my body; my bones have no soundness because of my sin."

Ps. 39:10   "Remove your scourge from me; I am overcome by the blow of your hand."

Ps. 44:2   "With your hand you drove out the nations . . . "

Ps. 59:5   "You, Lord God Almighty, you who are the God of Israel, rouse yourself to <u>punish</u> all the nations; show no mercy to wicked traitors."

Ps. 64:8   "He will turn their own tongues against them and bring them to ruin."

Ps. 89:32   "I will <u>punish</u> their sin with the rod, their iniquity with flogging."

Ps. 94:10   "Does he who disciplines nations not <u>punish</u>? Does he who teaches mankind lack knowledge?"

Ps. 99:8   "Lord our God, you answered them; you were to Israel a forgiving God, though you <u>punished</u> their misdeeds."

Ps. 99:10   "Does he who disciplines nations not <u>punish</u>?"

Ps. 119:84 "How long must your servant wait? When will you <u>punish</u> my persecutors?"

Ps. 120:4   "He will <u>punish</u> you with a warrior's sharp arrows, with burning coals of the broom bush."

a. Hebrew/Strong's/biblical use

- disciplines, to attend to, number, visit, to avenge, take vengeance, revenge, avenge one self, be avenged, be punished
- scourge: stroke, plague, disease
- to inoculate, sharp(en), teach diligently
- wrath: anger, indignation, rage

b. Other versions/translations

- anger
- beating
- bring about demise
- bring them to ruin
- correct
- defeated, destroy
- execute judgment
- judgment, judge
- make then stumble

- plague
- rage
- ruin, rebuke
- sickness, stroke
- took vengeance
- turn against them
- visit all
- wounding, weeded out

c. Praise & Prayer Journal

1. Give examples of who or what God punishes. (Answers include: the nations, their sins, their misdeeds, persecutors.)

2. What are biblical examples of this characteristic, attribute, or action of God? (Answers include: the people in Noah's day, before the flood; Sodom and Gomorrah; Pharaoh; Pharaoh's army while pursuing the Israelites; David and Bathsheba; those who improperly touched the ark of the covenant.)

3. When in your lifetime have you seen God punish? How?

73 **REBUKES**: God proves, decides, judges, destroys, corrects, commands, punishes, speaks, and gives stern warnings and reprimands.

Ps. 2:5   "Then he <u>rebukes</u> them in his anger . . . "

Ps. 6:1   "Lord, do not <u>rebuke</u> me in your anger or discipline me in your wrath."

Ps. 9:5   "You have <u>rebuked</u> the nations . . . "

Ps. 38:1   "O Lord, do not <u>rebuke</u> me in your anger or discipline me in your wrath."

Ps. 39:11   "You <u>rebuke</u> and discipline men for their sin."

Ps. 50:21   "But I will <u>rebuke</u> you and accuse you to your face."

Ps. 57:3   "He sends from heaven and saves me, <u>rebuking</u> those who hotly pursue me."

Ps. 76:6   "At your <u>rebuke</u>, God of Jacob, both horse and chariot lie still."

Ps. 80:16   "Your vine is cut down, it is burned with fire; at your <u>rebuke</u> your people perish."

Ps. 104:7   "But at your <u>rebuke</u> the water fled, at the sound of your thunder they took to flight."

Ps. 119:21   "You <u>rebuke</u> the arrogant, who are accursed, those who stray from your commands."

a. Hebrew/Strong's/biblical use

- a chiding, rebuke
- anger, heat, burning of anger
- reprimand, objection
- to perish, destroy
- to prove, decide, judge

b. Other versions/translations

- correct, condemned, command
- chasten, displeased
- punish
- reprove, roar, reprimand
- speaks
- speak to them, stern warnings
- terrified, shout
- threaten

c. Praise & Prayer Journal

1. What words are most often combined with God's rebuke? (Answers include: *anger, discipline*.)

2. Who or what does God rebuke? (Answers include: me, His people, the nations, the arrogant, the accursed, those who stray from His commands, even water, wind, and waves [by Jesus]!)

3. What are biblical examples of this characteristic, attribute, or action of God? (Answers include: Sodom and Gomorrah; God commanded the Red Sea and the Jordan River to part for the Israelites; the Israelite generation that built the golden calf as an idol; God rebuked Pharaoh, the prophets, and gods of Baal.)

4. When or how have you seen God rebuke? You? Your family? Others?

74   **REDEEMS**: God ransoms, rescues, delivers, gets me out of this, protects, saves, sets us free.

Ps. 34:22   "The LORD <u>redeems</u> his servants; no one will be condemned who takes refuge in him."

Ps. 49:15   "But God will <u>redeem</u> my life from the grave; he will surely take me to himself."

Ps. 77:15   "With your mighty arm you <u>redeemed</u> your people, the descendants of Jacob and Joseph."

Ps. 78:42   "They did not remember his power—the day he <u>redeemed</u> them from the oppressor."

Ps. 103:4   " . . . <u>redeems</u> your life from the pit."

Ps. 106:10   "He saved them from the hand of the foe; from the hand of the enemy he <u>redeemed</u> them."

Ps. 107:2   "Let the <u>redeemed</u> of the LORD tell their story—those he <u>redeemed</u> from the hand of the foe."

Ps. 119:134   "<u>Redeem</u> me from human oppression, that I may obey your precepts."

Ps. 119:154   "Defend my cause and <u>redeem</u> me; preserve my life according to your promise."

Ps. 130:8   "He himself will <u>redeem</u> Israel from all their sins."

a. Hebrew/Strong's/biblical use

- to ransom, to redeem
- to rescue, deliver

b. Other versions/translations

- defended, delivered
- freed
- get me out of this
- prays, protects

- rescues, ransom
- saves, snatches, sets free
- will buy me back

c. Praise & Prayer Journal

1. Who does God redeem? (Answers include: Israel, His servants, His people, me.)

2. From what does God redeem? (Answers include: the grave, pit, oppressor, the hand of the enemy or foe, human oppression, sins.)

3. What are biblical examples of this characteristic, attribute, or action of God? (Answers include: Joseph as a slave, and in prison; His people from slavery in Egypt; Moses and Joshua in their battles; Daniel in the lion's den.)

4. When has God redeemed you or members of your family?

75

REFRESHES: God leads, guides, establishes, prepares, restores, renews, and confirms.

Ps. 23:3   "He <u>refreshes</u> my soul. He guides me along the right paths for his name's sake."

Ps. 68:9   "You gave abundant showers, O God; you <u>refreshed</u> your weary inheritance."

a. Hebrew/Strong's/biblical use

- to be established, prepared
- to lead, guide (by implication, to transport)

b. Other versions/translations

- confirmed
- renews
- restores

c. Praise & Prayer Journal

1. Who does God refresh? (Answers could include: my soul, His weary inheritance, the soul of the sinful, the oppressed?)?

2. In what ways can we overlook God's refreshment? How might we notice and enjoy it more?

3. What are biblical examples of this characteristic, attribute, or action of God? (Answers could include: David refreshed Saul by playing the harp for him, Job after his trials, Jonah after being in the belly of the big fish, Elijah during and after his time of depression.)

4. When has God refreshed you and your family?

76

REFUGE: God is a defense, refuge, trust, shelter, retreat, place of safety, and a hiding place.

Ps. 7:1   "LORD my God, I take <u>refuge</u> in you; save and deliver me from all who pursue me."

Ps. 9:9   "The LORD is a <u>refuge</u> for the oppressed, a stronghold in times of trouble."

Ps. 11:1   "In the LORD I take <u>refuge</u> . . ."

Ps. 14:6	"... but the LORD is their <u>refuge</u>."
Ps. 16:1	"Keep me safe, O God, for in you I take <u>refuge</u>."
Ps. 17:7	"... those who take <u>refuge</u> in you and from their foes."
Ps. 18:2	"... in whom I take <u>refuge</u>."
Ps. 18:30	"... for all who take <u>refuge</u> in him."
Ps. 31:2	"... be my rock of <u>refuge</u>."
Ps. 31:4	"... for you are my <u>refuge</u>."
Ps. 34:8	"Blessed is the man who takes <u>refuge</u> in him."
Ps. 34:22	"The LORD will rescue his servants; no one who takes <u>refuge</u> in him will be condemned."
Ps. 36:7	"Both high and low among men find <u>refuge</u> in the shadow of your wings."
Ps. 37:40	"... because they take <u>refuge</u> in him."
Ps. 46:1	"God is our <u>refuge</u> and strength, an ever-present help in trouble."
Ps. 57:1	"I will take <u>refuge</u> in the shadow of your wings until the disaster has passed."
Ps. 59:16	"I will sing of your love; for you are my fortress, my <u>refuge</u> in times of trouble."
Ps. 61:3	"For you have been my <u>refuge</u>, a strong tower against the foe."
Ps. 61:4	"I long to dwell in your tent forever and take <u>refuge</u> in the shelter of your wings."
Ps. 62:7	"My salvation and my honor depend on God, he is my mighty rock, my <u>refuge</u>."
Ps. 62:8	"... for God is our <u>refuge</u>."
Ps. 64:10	"The righteous will rejoice in the LORD and take <u>refuge</u> in him; all the upright in heart will glory in him!"
Ps. 71:3	"Be my rock of <u>refuge</u> to which I can always go."
Ps. 71:7	"I have become a sign to many; you are my strong <u>refuge</u>."
Ps. 73:28	"But as for me, it is good to be near God. I have made the Sovereign LORD

my <u>refuge</u>; I will tell of all your deeds."

Ps. 91:2   "I will say of the LORD, 'He is my <u>refuge</u> and my fortress, my God, in whom I trust.'"

Ps. 91:4   "He will cover you with his feathers, and under his wings you will find <u>refuge</u>."

Ps. 91:9   "If you make the Most High your dwelling—even the LORD, who is my <u>refuge</u>."

Ps. 94:22   "But the LORD has become my fortress, and my God the rock in whom I take <u>refuge</u>."

Ps. 118:8   "It is better to take <u>refuge</u> in the LORD than to trust in man."

Ps. 118:9   "It is better to take <u>refuge</u> in the LORD than to trust in princes."

Ps. 119:114 "You are my <u>refuge</u> and my shield."

Ps. 142:5   "I cry to you, LORD; I say, 'You are my <u>refuge</u>, my portion in the land of the living.'"

Ps. 144:2   "He is my loving God and my fortress, my stronghold and my deliverer, my shield, in whom I take <u>refuge</u>, who subdues peoples under me."

a. Hebrew/Strong's/biblical use

- covering, shelter, hiding place, secrecy
- place or means of safety, protection, refuge, stronghold
- refuge, defense, high fort (tower)
- a retreat: den, dwelling place, habitation
- a shelter, hope (place of), refuge, shelter, trust
- to seek refuge, flee for protection, trust, hope in

b. Other versions/translations

- depend
- hide, hiding place
- protection, protect, place of safety
- quiet retreat
- strong habitation
- stronghold, safety, safe house, shelter
- trust
- when we run to Him

c. Praise & Prayer Journal

1. God provides refuge from what? (Answers include: our foes, times of trouble, oppression.)

2. Where do we find God's refuge? (Among the answers: in the shadow and the shelter under His wings.)

3. How else is God's refuge described or translated? (Among the answers: as our rock, a strong tower, as a fortress, protection, hiding place, safe house, and when we run to Him.)

4. What are biblical examples of this characteristic, attribute, or action of God? (Answers include: the Israelites in the desert; for Samuel; for David when being pursued by Saul, including hiding deep within the caves; for Jeremiah in his loneliness as the weeping prophet; protection for Nehemiah.)

5. When has God been your refuge?

77   RELIEVES: God allows to be quiet, tranquil, to be at peace, to rest, lie still, be undisturbed.

Ps. 4:1	"Give me <u>relief</u> from my distress . . . "
Ps. 94:13	" . . . <u>relief</u> from days of trouble."
Ps. 143:1	"Lᴏʀᴅ, hear my prayer, listen to my cry for mercy; in your faithfulness and righteousness come to my <u>relief</u>."

a. Hebrew/Strong's/biblical use

- rest, lie still, be undisturbed
- to be or grow wide, be or grow large
- to be quiet, be tranquil, be at peace

b. Other versions/translations

- enlarged
- free me
- help me
- protect
- rest

c. Praise & Prayer Journal

1. Under what conditions is relief from God granted? (Answers include: from my distress, from days of trouble, in response to a cry for mercy.)

2. What are biblical examples of this characteristic, attribute, or action of God? (Answers include: Joseph in the pit, Joseph as a slave in prison, Moses after he killed the Egyptian, for Samuel, David in his time of repentance, for Isaiah.)

3. When has God relieved you and your family from distress and days of trouble?

78   REMEMBERS: God accepts, is always thinking about us, looks favorably, remains loyal, and stands by us.

Ps. 20:3	"May he <u>remember</u> all your sacrifices . . . "
Ps. 25:6	<u>Remember</u>, LORD, your great mercy and love, for they are from of old."
Ps. 25:7	"Do not <u>remember</u> the sins of my youth and my rebellious ways; according to your love <u>remember</u> me, for you, LORD, are good."
Ps. 89:50	"<u>Remember</u>, LORD, how your servant has been mocked, how I bear in my heart the taunts of all the nations."
Ps. 98:3	"He has <u>remembered</u> his love and his faithfulness to Israel."
Ps. 105:8	"He <u>remembers</u> his covenant forever, the promise he made, for a thousand generations."
Ps. 105:42	"For he <u>remembered</u> his holy promise given to his servant Abraham."
Ps. 106:4	"<u>Remember</u> me, LORD, when you show favor to your people, come to my aid when you save them."

Ps. 106:45 "For their sake he <u>remembered</u> his covenant and out of his great love he relented."

Ps. 111:5 "He provides food for those who fear him; he <u>remembers</u> his covenant forever."

Ps. 115:12 "The LORD <u>remembers</u> us and will bless us: he will bless his people Israel, he will bless the house of Aaron."

Ps. 136:23 "He <u>remembered</u> us in our low estate."

a. Hebrew/Strong's/biblical use

- accept, anoint
- to remember

b. Other versions/translations

- accept; always thinking about us
- celebrate, consider
- hold against
- keep
- look favorably; look with favor
- mark the milestones; mindful of us

- regard with favor; remains loyal
- stands by
- takes a good look, takes note, takes notice of
- will ever be mindful of

c. Praise & Prayer Journal

1. What does God remember? (Answers include: His covenant forever, His love, His faithfulness, His holy promise, our sacrifices.)

2. Who does God remember? (Answers include: me, us, His servant Abraham, Israel.)

3. What are biblical examples of this characteristic, attribute, or action of God? (Answers include: saving Noah and his family in the ark; Abraham's request to save Lot and his family; giving Abraham and Sarah a child as promised; Rachel's womb being opened; Hannah's request for a child and the Lord remembering her with the birth of Samuel.)

4. What should you praise God for when He remembers your prayers and requests?

79

RESCUES: God rescues, delivers, frees, protects, redeems, saves, and provides escape.

Ps. 17:13	"Rescue me from the wicked by your sword."
Ps. 18:17	"He rescued me from my powerful enemy."
Ps. 18:19	"He brought me out into a spacious place; he rescued me because he delighted in me."
Ps. 18:48	"You exalted me above my foes; from a violent man you rescued me."
Ps. 22:8	" . . . let the LORD rescue him."
Ps. 22:21	"Rescue me from the mouth of the lions . . . "
Ps. 34:22	"The LORD will rescue his servants; no one who takes refuge in him will be condemned."
Ps. 35:10	"You rescue the poor from those too strong for them."
Ps. 35:17	"How long, LORD, will you look on? Rescue me from their ravages, my precious life from these lions."
Ps. 43:1	" . . . rescue me from deceitful and wicked men."
Ps. 44:26	"Rise up and help us; rescue us because of your unfailing love."
Ps. 55:18	"He rescues me unharmed from the battle waged against me, even though many oppose me."
Ps. 69:14	"Rescue me from the mire, do not let me sink; deliver me from those who hate me, from the deep waters."
Ps. 69:18	"Come near and rescue me; deliver me because of my foes."
Ps. 71:2	"In your righteousness rescue me and deliver me; turn your ear to me and save me."
Ps. 72:14	"He will rescue them from oppression and violence, for precious is their blood in his sight."
Ps. 81:7	"In your distress you called and I rescued you."

Ps. 82:4   "<u>Rescue</u> the weak and needy . . ."

Ps. 91:14   "'Because he loves me,' says the Lᴏʀᴅ, 'I will <u>rescue</u> him.'"

Ps. 107:20   "He sent out his word and healed them; he <u>rescued</u> them from the grave."

Ps. 113:7   "He raises the poor from the dust and lifts the needy."

Ps. 140:1   "<u>Rescue</u> me, Lᴏʀᴅ, from evildoers; protect me from the violent."

Ps. 142:6   "Listen to my cry, for I am in desperate need; <u>rescue</u> me from those who pursue me, for they are too strong for me."

Ps. 143:9   "<u>Rescue</u> me from my enemies, Lᴏʀᴅ, for I hide myself in you."

Ps. 144:7   "Reach down your hand from on high; deliver me and <u>rescue</u> me from the mighty waters, from the hands of foreigners."

Ps. 144:11   "Deliver me; <u>rescue</u> me from the hands of foreigners, whose mouths are full of lies, whose right hands are deceitful."

a. Hebrew/Strong's/biblical use

- be high
- escape, save, deliver, slip away
- remove, draw out, draw off, withdraw
- rise, stand
- to arm for war
- to deliver, rescue
- to equip (for war)
- to ransom, rescue, deliver

b. Other versions/translations

- deliver
- frees
- got you out of a bad place
- picks up
- protects, pulled you back
- redeems, ransom
- rescues
- saved, saves
- sets free
- snatch

c. Praise & Prayer Journal

1. Who does God rescue? (Answers include: me, us, His servants, the poor, the weak, the needy.)

2. Who does God rescue us from? (Answers include: the wicked, powerful enemies, the mouths of lions, those too strong, the deceitful, foes, evildoers, those who pursue me, hands of foreigners.)

3. What does God rescue us from? (Answers include: ravages, the battles waged against me, oppressive violence, the grave, mighty waters.)

4. What are biblical examples of this characteristic, attribute, or action of God? (Answers include: the Israelites in Egypt; Rahab and her family, saved when Jericho's walls fell; from Goliath and the Philistines; the Jewish people from the king of Assyria; Daniel in the lion's den; Jonah from drowning, the big fish actually saving him.)

5. Who or what has God rescued you and your family from?

 RESTORES: God returns, blesses, brings back, heals, helps us again, makes us well and new again, turns life around, and brings good times back.

Ps. 14:7	"When the LORD <u>restores</u> the fortunes of his people, let Jacob rejoice."
Ps. 41:3	"The LORD sustains them on their sickbed and <u>restores</u> them from their bed of illness."
Ps. 51:12	"<u>Restore</u> to me the joy of your salvation and grant me a willing spirit, to sustain me."
Ps. 53:6	"When God <u>restores</u> the fortunes of his people, let Jacob rejoice and Israel be glad!"
Ps. 60:1	"You have rejected us, God, and burst upon us; you have been angry—now <u>restore</u> us!"
Ps. 71:20	"Though you have made me see troubles, many and bitter, you will <u>restore</u> my life again."
Ps. 80:3	"<u>Restore</u> us, O God; make your face shine on us, that we may be saved."
Ps. 80:7	"<u>Restore</u> us, God Almighty; make your face shine on us, that we may be saved."

Ps. 80:19   "<u>Restore</u> us, LORD God Almighty; make your face shine on us, that we may be saved."

Ps. 85:1   "You, LORD, showed favor to your land; you <u>restored</u> the fortunes of Jacob."

Ps. 85:4   "<u>Restore</u> us again, God our Savior, and put away your displeasure toward us."

Ps. 126:1   "When the LORD <u>restored</u> the fortunes of Zion, we were like those who dreamed."

Ps. 126:4   "<u>Restore</u> our fortunes, LORD, like streams in the Negev."

a. Hebrew/Strong's/biblical use

- to return
- to turn back

b. Other versions/translations

- bless, blessed
- bring back, bring me up, brought back
- brought good times back
- give back
- heals
- helps us again
- makes well, makes us new again
- sustains
- turns life around, turns back, turn us again

c. Praise & Prayer Journal

1. Who does God restore? (Answers include: His people, me, us.)

2. What does God restore? (Answers include: the joy of salvation, life, fortunes, from our illness, my life again.)

3. What are biblical examples of this characteristic, attribute, or action of God? (Answers include: Joseph from slavery and prison, Job following his great losses, rebuilding the cities of Judah, restoring the tents of Jacob, King David's restoration of the fortunes of his peoples Israel [Amos 9:14].)

4. When has God restored you and your family?

81   **REWARDS**: God pays back, restores, rewards, and repays.

Ps. 18:20   "The LORD has dealt with me according to my righteousness; according to the cleanness of my hands he has <u>rewarded</u> me."

Ps. 18:24   "The LORD has <u>rewarded</u> me according to my righteousness."

Ps. 62:12   "You <u>reward</u> everyone according to what they have done."

a. Hebrew/Strong's/biblical use

- to return
- to turn back

b. Other versions/translations

- paid me back
- recompensed, restored
- render, repay

c. Praise & Prayer Journal

1. On what basis does God reward? (Answers could include: according to the cleanness of my hands, according to my righteousness, according to what we have done.)

2. What are biblical examples of this characteristic, attribute, or action of God? (Answers include: Abraham and Sarah through the birth of their son, Isaac; Abraham's inheritance; Jacob's allotment of his inheritance; Solomon with wisdom after he humbled himself in his request before God.)

3. How has God rewarded you and your family?

82

RIGHTEOUS: God is just, lawful, completely fair and right, faithful, fair, honest; He makes things right, is trustworthy, and absolutely just.

Ps. 4:1 "Answer me when I call to you, my <u>righteous</u> God. Give me relief from my distress; have mercy on me and hear my prayer."

Ps. 7:9 " . . . you, the <u>righteous</u> God who probes minds and hearts."

Ps. 7:11 "God is a <u>righteous</u> judge, a God who displays his wrath every day."

Ps. 7:17 "I will give thanks to the Lord because of his <u>righteousness</u>; I will sing the praises of the name of the Lord Most High."

Ps. 9:4 "For you have upheld my right and my cause, sitting enthroned as the <u>righteous</u> judge."

Ps. 9:8 "He rules the world in <u>righteousness</u> and judges the peoples with equity."

Ps. 11:7 "For the Lord is <u>righteous</u>, he loves justice; the upright will see his face."

Ps. 19:9 "The decrees of the Lord are firm, and all of them are <u>righteous</u>."

Ps. 35:28 "My tongue will proclaim your <u>righteousness</u>, your praises all day long."

Ps. 36:6 "Your righteousness is like the mighty mountains . . . "

Ps. 48:10 "Like your name, O God, your praise reaches to the ends of the earth; your right hand is filled with <u>righteousness</u>."

Ps. 65:5 "You answer us with awesome and <u>righteous</u> deeds, God our Savior."

Ps. 71:2 "In your <u>righteousness</u>, rescue me and deliver me; turn your ear to me and save me."

Ps. 71:15 "My mouth will tell of your <u>righteous</u> deeds, of your saving acts all day long."

Ps. 71:16 "I will come and proclaim your mighty acts, Sovereign Lord; I will proclaim your <u>righteous</u> deeds, yours alone."

Ps. 71:19 "Your <u>righteousness</u>, God, reaches to the heavens, you who have done great things. Who is like you, God?"

Ps. 71:24	"My tongue will tell of your <u>righteous</u> acts all day long, for those who wanted to harm me have been put to shame and confusion."
Ps. 85:11	"Faithfulness springs forth from the earth, and <u>righteousness</u> looks down from heaven."
Ps. 88:12	"Are your wonders known in the place of darkness, or your <u>righteous</u> deeds in the land of oblivion?"
Ps. 89:14	"<u>Righteousness</u> and justice are the foundation of your throne."
Ps. 89:16	" . . . they celebrate your <u>righteousness</u>."
Ps. 97:2	"Clouds and thick darkness surround him; <u>righteousness</u> and justice are the foundation of his throne."
Ps. 97:6	"The heavens proclaim his <u>righteousness</u>, and all peoples see his glory."
Ps. 103:6	"The LORD works <u>righteousness</u> and justice for all the oppressed."
Ps. 103:17	"But from everlasting to everlasting the LORD's love is with those who fear him, and his <u>righteousness</u> with their children's children."
Ps. 111:3	"Glorious and majestic are his deeds, and his <u>righteousness</u> endures forever."
Ps. 119:142	"Your <u>righteousness</u> is everlasting and your law is true."

a. Hebrew/Strong's/biblical use

- justice, righteousness
- just, lawful

b. Other versions/translations

- completely fair; completely right
- does what is right; has done what is right
- equity
- faithful, fair, fairly, fairness
- goodness in action
- honest; holiness
- just; justice
- makes things right; makes everything come out right
- putting things right

- righteous altogether; right
- solemn honor; saving acts
- trustworthy and absolutely just
- victory
- wonderful things

c. Praise & Prayer Journal

1. How is God's righteousness described? (Answers include: like the mighty mountains, it reaches to the heavens, by His acts and deeds, everlasting, enduring forever.)

2. What other characteristics are disclosed with righteousness? (Answers include: He loves justice, judges people with equity, is a righteous judge, looks down from Heaven.)

3. What are biblical examples of this characteristic, attribute, or action of God? (Answers include: Abraham's intercession and plea for Lot and his family in Sodom; Pharaoh finally relenting to Moses and Aaron and saying that he has sinned and the Lord is the righteous one; His covenant to give His people the promised land from their enemies; The Levitical priests and the prophets witnessing God's righteousness; God judging the Israelites for their sins; "There is no other God besides me, a righteous God, a Savior, there is none except me" [Isaiah].)

4. When has God exhibited what is right, just, and fair, and done wonderful things in your life and for your family?

83

ROCK: God as a protector, is also rock solid, strong, and can be sheltering; He is your rock of refuge and your salvation.

Ps. 18:2   "The LORD is my <u>rock</u> . . . My God is my rock."

Ps. 18:31   "For who is God besides the LORD? And who is the <u>rock</u> except our God?"

Ps. 18:46   "The LORD lives! Praise be to my <u>rock</u>! Exalted be God my Savior!"

Ps. 19:14   "May these words of my mouth and this meditation of my heart be pleasing in your sight, LORD, my <u>rock</u> and my redeemer."

Ps. 28:1   "To you I call, O LORD my <u>rock</u>."

Ps. 31:2   " . . . be my <u>rock</u> of refuge."

Ps. 31:3   "Since you are my <u>rock</u> and my fortress, for the sake of your name lead and guide me."

Ps. 42:9   "I say to God my <u>rock</u> . . . "

Ps. 62:2   "He alone is my <u>rock</u> and my salvation; he is my fortress, I will never be shaken."

Ps. 62:6   "Truly he is my <u>rock</u> and my salvation; he is my fortress, I will not be shaken."

Ps. 62:7   "My salvation and my honor depend on God; he is my mighty <u>rock</u>, my refuge."

Ps. 71:3   "Be my <u>rock</u> of refuge to which I can always go."

Ps. 78:35   "They remembered that God was their <u>rock</u>, that God Most High was their redeemer."

Ps. 89:26   "You are my Father, my God, the <u>rock</u>, my Savior."

Ps. 92:15   "The LORD is upright; he is my <u>rock</u>."

Ps. 94:22   "My God the <u>rock</u> in whom I take refuge."

Ps. 95:1   "Come, let us sing for joy to the LORD; let us shout aloud to the <u>rock</u> of our salvation."

Ps. 144:1   "Praise be to the LORD my <u>rock</u>, who trains my hands for war, my fingers for battle."

a. Hebrew/Strong's/biblical use

• rock, cliff

b. Other versions/translations

• bedrock
• granite cave

- high ridge, high mountain retreat
- mountain
- protector
- rock solid
- strength, sheltering rock, strong

c. Praise & Prayer Journal

1. Explain God's actions and attributes: as protector, through His strength, through His sheltering.

2. What other attributes are included with rock? (Most often, from the Psalms: refuge, fortress, salvation.)

3. Who in the Bible relied on God to be their rock? (Among the numerous answers: Noah, Moses, David, Job.)

4. What are other biblical examples of this characteristic, attribute, or action of God? (Answers include: Samuel refers to the God as "the rock of Israel," nor is there "any other rock like our God"; "Is there any other rock?" [Isaiah].)

5. When has God been a rock in your life and the life of your family?

84   SAVES: God helps, rescues, sets everything right, pulls me from—and lifts me above—troubles; He is our Savior.

Ps. 7:1   "O LORD . . . <u>save</u> and deliver me from all who pursue me."

Ps. 7:10   "My shield is God Most High, who <u>saves</u> the upright in heart."

Ps. 17:7   " . . . you who <u>save</u> by your right hand."

Ps. 18:16   "He drew me out of deep waters."

Ps. 18:27   "You <u>save</u> the humble . . . "

Ps. 18:48   " . . . who <u>saves</u> me from my enemies."

Ps. 20:6	"Now I know that the LORD <u>saves</u> his anointed . . . with the saving power of his right hand."
Ps. 22:5	"They cried to you and were <u>saved</u> . . . "
Ps. 34:6	"This poor man called, and the LORD hears him; he saved him out of all his troubles."
Ps. 34:18	"The LORD . . . <u>saves</u> those who are crushed in spirit."
Ps. 37:40	"The LORD helps them and delivers them; he delivers them from the wicked and <u>saves</u> them, because they take refuge in him."
Ps. 51:14	"<u>Save</u> me from bloodguilt, O God, the God who <u>saves</u> me."
Ps. 54:1	"<u>Save</u> me, O God, by your name; vindicate me by your might."
Ps. 55:16	"As for me, I call to God, and the LORD <u>saves</u> me."
Ps. 57:3	"He sends from heaven and <u>saves</u> me, rebuking those who hotly pursue me—God sends forth his love and his faithfulness."
Ps. 68:20	"Our God is a God who <u>saves</u>; from the Sovereign LORD comes escape from death."
Ps. 70:1	"Hasten, O God, to <u>save</u> me . . . "
Ps. 80:3	"Restore us, O God; make your face shine on us, that we may be <u>saved</u>."
Ps. 88:1	"LORD you are the God who <u>saves</u> me; day and night I cry out to you."
Ps. 106:8	"Yet he <u>saved</u> them for his name's sake, to make his mighty power known."
Ps. 106:10	"He <u>saved</u> them from the hand of the foe; from the hand of the enemy he redeemed them."
Ps. 106:21	"They forgot the God who <u>saved</u> them, who had done great things in Egypt."
Ps. 107:13	"Then they cried to the LORD in their trouble, and he <u>saved</u> them from their distress."
Ps. 116:6	"The LORD protects the unwary; when I was brought low, he <u>saved</u> me."
Ps. 145:19	"He fulfills the desires of those who fear him; he hears their cry and <u>saves</u> them."

a. Hebrew/Strong's/biblical use

- helper, rescuer, savior
- to deliver, rescue
- to escape, save/deliver, slip away

b. Other versions/translations

- deliver, delivers, delivered, deliverance
- forgive
- give victory; gave it; got me out
- lift me above
- pulled me from
- rescue; rescued; rescues
- righteous deeds
- saves; salvation; savior
- set everything right
- take the side of

c. Praise & Prayer Journal

1. Whom does God save? (Answers include: His anointed, the upright in heart, the humble crushed in spirit, those who fear Him.)

2. God saves from whom and what? (Answers include: all who pursue me, my enemies, out of our troubles, the wicked, the foe, the hand of the enemy, from distress.)

3. Who did God save in the Bible? (Answers include: His people, David while Absalom was pursuing him, Job, Jeremiah when he was lowered into a pit, Daniel in the lion's den.)

4. What are other biblical examples of this characteristic, attribute, or action of God? (Answers include: Noah and his family in the flood; Hagar and Ishmael, when Sarah sent them to the desert; the Israelites in Egypt; David from the pit of destruction as Saul was pursuing him.)

5. When and under what circumstances has God saved you, your family, your friends?

85

SAVIOR: God delivers, rescues, intervenes, protects, and shelters.

Ps. 24:5	"He will receive blessing from the LORD and vindication from God his <u>Savior</u>."
Ps. 25:5	"For you are God my <u>Savior</u>, and my hope is in you all day long."
Ps. 27:1	"The LORD is my light and my <u>salvation</u> . . ."
Ps. 27:9	"Do not reject me or forsake me, O God my <u>Savior</u>."
Ps. 28:8	" . . . a fortress of <u>salvation</u> for his anointed one."
Ps. 35:3	"Say to my soul, 'I am your <u>salvation</u>.'"
Ps. 37:39	"The <u>salvation</u> of the righteous comes from the LORD."
Ps. 37:40	"He delivers them from the wicked and <u>saves</u> them."
Ps. 38:22	"Come quickly to help me, O LORD my <u>Savior</u>."
Ps. 40:13	"Be pleased, O LORD, to <u>save</u> me . . ."
Ps. 42:5	"Put your hope in God, for I will yet praise him, my <u>Savior</u> and my God."
Ps. 42:11	"Why, my soul, are you downcast? Why so disturbed within me? Put your hope in God, for I will yet praise him, my <u>Savior</u> and my God."
Ps. 43:5	"Put your hope in God, for I will yet praise Him, my <u>Savior</u> and my God."
Ps. 50:23	" . . . so that I may show Him the <u>salvation</u> of God."
Ps. 53:6	"Oh, that <u>salvation</u> for Israel would come out of Zion!"
Ps. 55:16	"But I call to God, and the LORD <u>saves</u> me."
Ps. 57:3	"He sends from heaven and <u>saves</u> me."
Ps. 65:5	"You answer us with awesome and righteous deeds, God our <u>Savior</u>, the hope of all the ends of the earth and of the farthest seas."
Ps. 68:19	"Praise be to the LORD, to God our <u>Savior</u>, who daily bears our burdens."
Ps. 79:9	"Help us, God our <u>Savior</u>, for the glory of your name; deliver us and forgive our sins for your name's sake."
Ps. 85:4	"Restore us again, God our <u>Savior</u>, and put away your displeasure toward us."

Ps. 88:1	"O Lᴏʀᴅ, the God who <u>saves</u> me . . . "
Ps. 89:26	"You are my Father, my God, the rock, my <u>Savior</u>."
Ps. 91:3	"Surely he will <u>save</u> you from the fowler's snare and from the deadly pestilence."
Ps. 107:19	"They cried to the Lᴏʀᴅ in their trouble, and he <u>saved</u> them from their distress."

a. Hebrew/Strong's/biblical use

- deliverance, salvation, rescue, safety, welfare
- to deliver, rescue

b. Other versions/translations

- delivers me, deliverer
- health or help of my countenance
- intervene
- protection; power to deliver
- rescue
- salvation, saves me; saving strength; saving defense, saving intervention
- saving refuge; shelters; safety
- take refuge in, trust
- vindicates me

c. Praise & Prayer Journal

1. Who does God save? (Answers include: me, you, those who are righteous.)

2. Do you look at God as your savior? Personal savior? What might help you to do that?

3. What are biblical examples of this characteristic, attribute, or action of God? (Answers include: Abraham, Isaac, Jacob, Joseph, God was savior to Moses and His people, the judges, David, Isaiah.)

4. When has God, as a savior, sheltered you and your family from evil, distress, and the wicked?

86

SHELTERS: God provides a hiding place, secret place, safe house, secure place, and protects us.

Ps. 27:5   "For in the day of trouble he will keep me safe in his dwelling; he will hide me in the <u>shelter</u> of his sacred tent and set me high upon a rock."

Ps. 31:20   "In the <u>shelter</u> of your presence you hide them from all human intrigues; you keep them safe in your dwelling from accusing tongues."

Ps. 61:4   "I long to dwell in your tent forever and take refuge in the <u>shelter</u> of your wings."

Ps. 91:1   "He who dwells in the <u>shelter</u> of the Most High will rest in the shadow of the Almighty."

a. Hebrew/Strong's/biblical use

- covering, shelter
- hiding place, secrecy

b. Other versions/translations

- covert
- pavilion
- secret place, safe, safe house

- secure place, sanctuary
- shadow
- tent

c. Praise & Prayer Journal

1. Where is God's shelter described? (Among the answers: His sacred tent, His presence, His wings, of the Most High.)

2. What are other biblical examples of this characteristic, attribute, or action of God? (Answers include: Noah and his family in the ark; David hiding from Saul deep within the caves and other hiding spots; great prophets like Isaiah, Jeremiah, and Nehemiah finding their hiding places in God.)

3. When has God sheltered you and your family, providing a hiding, secret, or secure place?

87

SHEPHERD: God tends, feeds, and cares for us.

Ps. 23:1   "The LORD is my <u>shepherd</u>, I lack nothing."

Ps. 28:9   "Save your people and bless your inheritance; be their <u>shepherd</u> and carry them forever."

Ps. 80:1   "Hear us, <u>Shepherd</u> of Israel, you who lead Joseph like a flock. You who sit enthroned between the cherubim, shine forth."

Ps. 95:7   "We are the people of his <u>pasture</u>."

a. Hebrew/Strong's/biblical use

- to pasture
- to tend

b. Other versions/translations

- care for them
- feed them

c. Praise & Prayer Journal

1. Who personally has God been a shepherd for? (Answers include: me, us, Israel, David, the prophets.)

2. What are biblical examples of this characteristic, attribute, or action of God? (Answers include: Moses and Aaron leading God's people, the Israelites in the desert, Naomi and Ruth, the Israelites during times of famine, David as shepherd among the sheep, David as shepherd of his people Israel.)

3. Name some times God has been a shepherd for you and your family, tending and caring for you?

88

SHIELDS: God protects, defends, covers over, provides armor, and keeps us safe.

Ps. 3:3   "But you are a <u>shield</u> around me . . . "

Ps. 5:12   "Surely, Lord, you bless the righteous; you surround them with your favor as with a <u>shield</u>."

Ps. 7:10   "My <u>shield</u> is God Most High, who saves the upright in heart."

Ps. 18:2   "The Lord is my rock, my fortress, and my deliverer; my God is my rock, in whom I take refuge. He is my <u>shield</u> and the horn of my salvation, my stronghold."

Ps. 18:30   "The Lord's word is flawless; he <u>shields</u> all who take refuge in him."

Ps. 18:35   "You make your saving help my <u>shield</u> and your right hand sustains me; your help has made me great."

Ps. 28:7   "The Lord is my strength and my <u>shield</u>."

Ps. 33:20   "We wait in hope for the Lord; he is our help and our <u>shield</u>."

Ps. 35:2   "Take up <u>shield</u> and buckler . . . Brandish spear and javelin . . . "

Ps. 59:11   "But do not kill them, O Lord our <u>shield</u>."

Ps. 84:11   "For the Lord God is a sun and <u>shield</u>."

Ps. 89:18   "Indeed, our <u>shield</u> belongs to the Lord."

Ps. 91:4   "His faithfulness will be your <u>shield</u> and rampart."

Ps. 115:9   "All you Israelites, trust in the Lord —he is their help and <u>shield</u>."

Ps. 115:10 "House of Aaron, trust in the Lord—he is their help and <u>shield</u>."

Ps. 115:11 "Trust in the Lord—he is their help and <u>shield</u>."

Ps. 119:114 "You are my refuge and my <u>shield</u>; I have put my hope in your word."

Ps. 140:7   "Sovereign Lord, my strong deliverer, you <u>shield</u> my head in the day of battle."

Ps. 144:2   "He is my loving God and my fortress, my stronghold and my deliverer, my <u>shield</u>, in whom I take refuge, who subdues peoples under me."

a. Hebrew/Strong's/biblical use

- buckle hook, shield, target
- cover over, protect, defend
- hedge in, join together
- the scaly hide of the crocodile

b. Other versions/translations

- armor
- covered
- defense
- keeps us safe
- protection; protector
- protective shield; protects me

c. Praise & Prayer Journal

1. Who is our shield? (Answers include: God Most High, the LORD, the LORD God, the sovereign LORD, our loving God.)

2. How, and from what, does God shield us? (Answers include: around me, surround them, take refuge in Him, saving help, our shield, shield my head.)

3. What are biblical examples of this characteristic, attribute, or action of God? (Answers include: Noah and his family and all the animals, Abraham in his travels, Moses, Joshua, David, the Israelites being shielded from their many enemies [including Pharaoh and his army].)

4. When has God shielded you and your family, including being a saving help, rock, fortress or refuge, or providing an armor and defense?

89 SILENCES: God cuts off, destroys, gets rid of, shuts up, or stops.

Ps. 12:3   "May the LORD <u>silence</u> all flattering lips and every boastful tongue."

Ps. 63:11   "But the king will rejoice in God; all who swear by God will glory in him, while the mouths of liars will be <u>silenced</u>."

Ps. 101:8   "I will put to <u>silence</u> all the wicked."

Ps. 143:12   "In your unfailing love, <u>silence</u> my enemies; destroy all my foes, for I am your servant."

a. Hebrew/Strong's/biblical use

- consume, cut off, destroy, vanish
- stop, give over

- to cut, cut off
- to perish, destroy

b. Other versions/translations

- cut off
- destroy
- ferret out
- get rid of

- purge
- shut; shut up, stopped
- vanquish

c. Praise & Prayer Journal

1. Who does God silence? (Answers include: the mouths of liars, all the wicked, my enemies.)

2. What can God silence? (Answers include: flattering lips, every boastful tongue.)

3. What are biblical examples of this characteristic, attribute, or action of God? (Answers include: Balaam's talking donkey stopping the journey, David's enemies, Zechariah for his disbelief of Elizabeth having a child at their age.)

4. Has God ever silenced you, your family, or your friends? Your adversaries and enemies?

90   SOVEREIGN: God is Almighty, King, and Lord God.

Ps. 47:2   "How awesome is the LORD Most High, the great king over all the earth."

Ps. 47:7   "For God is the King of all the earth."

Ps. 68:20   "Our God is a God who saves; from the <u>Sovereign</u> Lord comes escape from death."

Ps. 71:5   "For you have been my hope, <u>Sovereign</u> Lord, my confidence since my youth."

Ps. 71:16   "I will come and proclaim your mighty acts, <u>Sovereign</u> Lord; I will proclaim your righteous deeds, yours alone."

Ps. 73:28   "But as for me, it is good to be near God. I have made the <u>Sovereign</u> Lord my refuge; I will tell of all your deeds."

Ps. 109:21   "But you, <u>Sovereign</u> Lord, help me for your name's sake; out of the goodness of your love, deliver me."

Ps. 140:7   "<u>Sovereign</u> Lord, my strong deliverer, you shield my head in the day of battle."

Ps. 141:8   "But my eyes are fixed on you, <u>Sovereign</u> Lord; in you I take refuge—do not give me over to death."

a Hebrew/Strong's/biblical use

- God, Mighty
- Yahweh, Jehovah, Lord (the sacred and exclusive name of Almighty God)

b. Other versions/translations

- Almighty
- God
- King
- Lord God

c. Praise & Prayer Journal:

1. Why is "Lord" always listed with sovereignty? (Among the answers: It means Yahweh, Jehovah, Lord, the sacred and exclusive name of God and Almighty God; God is Lord of the hosts, the Holy One, the Lord most high, the Lord sits as king forever, the Lord reigns, King of the Nations, King of Kings, Lord of Lords; the Almighty, God of Heaven, God of earth, the Lord sitting on the throne, the throne of God, He sits above the circle of the earth.)

2. What are biblical examples of this characteristic, attribute, or action of God? (Among

the answers: God's covenant with Abraham, God's communications with Moses, the burning bush, the Ten Commandments, God's sovereignty is displayed in the contest between Elijah and the priests of Baal.)

3. What are benefits we reap from our LORD being sovereign? (Answers include: He is our refuge, He provides our escape from death.)

4. Does God control everything? Can He do anything, above and superior to all others?

91 SPEAKS: God commands, calls, talks, answers, and appoints.

Ps. 33:9   "For he <u>spoke</u>, and it came to be; he commanded, and it stood firm."

Ps. 50:7   "Hear, O my people, and I will <u>speak</u> . . . I will testify against you: I am God, your God."

Ps. 99:7   "He <u>spoke</u> to them from the pillar of cloud; they kept his statutes and the decrees he gave them."

Ps. 107:25   "For he <u>spoke</u> and stirred up a tempest that lifted high the waves."

a. Hebrew/Strong's/biblical use

- to say, answer, appoint, avouch, bid, call, certify, challenge
- to speak, say, talk

b. Other versions/translations

- commanded, commands

c. Praise & Prayer Journal

1. In the Bible, when God spoke, what happened? (Answers include: what He spoke came to be, things were stirred up.)

2. What are biblical examples of this characteristic, attribute, or action of God? (Answers include: the creation of Adam and Eve, His commands given to Noah, His covenant with Abraham, Moses and the Ten Commandments, when He spoke to Gideon during Gideon's fleece test, to Elijah through a small whisper, when He commanded Jonah, during the time John the Baptist baptized Jesus, through many dreams and visions. In addition, we can deduce from the Bible that God spoke directly to more than twenty people, including: Cain, Noah, Noah and his sons, Job and his friends, Abimelech, Isaac, Jacob, Joshua, Samuel, David, Nathan, Solomon, Jehu, Elijah, Isaiah, Ahaz, Manasseh, Jonah, Ezekiel, Hosea, Haggai, Zechariah, at the baptism of Jesus, Jesus at the transfiguration.)

3. When have you believed that God has commanded, called, or appointed you and your family to do or say something?

92 SPLENDOR: God has majesty, beauty, glory, magnificence, honor, holy array, and attire.

Ps. 29:2 "Ascribe to the LORD the glory due his name; worship the LORD in the splendor of his holiness."

Ps. 71:8 "My mouth is filled with your praise, declaring your splendor all day long."

Ps. 90:16 "May your deeds be shown to your servants, your splendor to their children."

Ps. 96:6 "Splendor and majesty are before him; strength and glory are in his sanctuary."

Ps. 104:1 "Praise the LORD, my soul. LORD my God, you are very great; you are clothed with splendor and majesty."

Ps. 145:5 "They speak of the glorious splendor of your majesty—and I will meditate on your wonderful works."

Ps. 145:12 " . . . so that all people may know of your mighty acts and the glorious splendor of your kingdom."

Ps. 148:13   "Let them praise the name of the Lord, for his name alone is exalted; his <u>splendor</u> is above the earth and the heavens."

a. Hebrew/Strong's/biblical use

- beauty, splendor, glory
- decoration: beauty, honor
- ornament, splendor, honor, majesty, glory
- splendor, majesty, vigor

b. Other versions/translations

- beauty
- glory, glorious power
- holy array, holy attire, honor
- magnificent

c Praise & Prayer Journal

1. How is splendor described along with God? (Answers include: His holiness, majesty, and kingdom.)

2. Who saw the splendor of God? (Answers include: Moses, Daniel, Ezekiel, John in Revelation.)

3. What are other biblical examples of this characteristic, attribute, or action of God? (Answers include: Moses receiving the Ten Commandments on Mount Sinai; Isaiah's description of the wonderful splendor of the Lord our God and God's sacred highway [Isaiah 35]; in Revelation, the description of God in Heaven and Jesus as the exalted Christ.)

4. What things on earth evoke God's splendor and majesty? (Among numerous answers: magnificent sunrises and sunsets.)

93

STRENGTH: God helps, supports, assists, praises, and is powerful; He is strong like a foundation that is rock-firm and stable.

Ps. 18:32	"It is God who arms me with <u>strength</u> . . . "
Ps. 21:13	"Be exalted in your <u>strength</u>, Lord; we will sing and praise your might."
Ps. 22:19	"O my <u>Strength</u>, come quickly to help me."
Ps. 28:7	"The Lord is my <u>strength</u> and my shield . . . "
Ps. 28:8	"The Lord is the <u>strength</u> of his people . . . "
Ps. 29:1	"Ascribe to the Lord, you heavenly beings, ascribe to the Lord glory and <u>strength</u>."
Ps. 44:3	"It was not by their sword. . . . It was your right hand, your arm . . . "
Ps. 46:1	"God is our refuge and <u>strength</u>, an ever-present help in trouble."
Ps. 59:9	"You are my <u>strength</u>, I watch for you; you, God, are my fortress."
Ps. 59:16	"But I will sing of your <u>strength</u>, in the morning I will sing of your love; for you are my fortress, my refuge in times of trouble."
Ps. 59:17	"You are my <u>strength</u>, I sing praise to you; you, God, are my fortress, my God on whom I can rely."
Ps. 68:28	"Summon your power, God; show us your <u>strength</u>, O God, as you have done before."
Ps. 68:35	"You, God, are awesome in your sanctuary; the God of Israel gives power and <u>strength</u> to his people. Praise be to God!"
Ps. 73:26	"My flesh and my heart may fail, but God is the <u>strength</u> of my heart."
Ps. 81:1	"Sing for joy to God our <u>strength</u>; shout aloud to the God of Jacob!"
Ps. 93:1	" . . . armed with <u>strength</u>."
Ps. 96:6	"Splendor and majesty are before him; <u>strength</u> and glory are in his sanctuary."
Ps. 96:7	"Ascribe to the Lord, all you families of nations, ascribe to the Lord glory and <u>strength</u>."

Ps. 105:4   "Look to the LORD and his <u>strength</u>."

Ps. 118:14   "The LORD is my <u>strength</u> and my song."

a. Hebrew/Strong's/biblical use

- boldness, loud, might, majesty
- a help, support, an assistance
- praise, power, strength, strong
- strength and security
- strength, might, wealth, army

b. Other versions/translations

- foundation
- help
- mighty
- power, prowess, powerful
- rock firm
- stability
- strong

c. Praise & Prayer Journal

1. What is described as alongside God's strength? (Answers include: His glory, He gives power and strength to His people.)

2. How is God's strength personalized for me, for us? (Answers include: He arms me with strength, the LORD is my strength, the strength of my heart, He is a fortress [used three times with *strength* in the Psalms], and a refuge [used with *strength* two times].)

3. What are biblical examples of this characteristic, attribute, or action of God? (Answers include: Moses and the Israelites being saved from the Egyptian army, Samuel, Isaiah, Nehemiah, Zechariah; and those who wait for the LORD shall renew their strength [Isaiah 40:31].)

4. For you and your family, when has God been your refuge, fortress, a rock-firm and stable foundation?

94

STRONG: God is mighty and powerful, a stronghold providing strength and security, and a house of defense.

Ps. 24:8   "Who is this King of glory? The LORD <u>strong</u> and mighty, the LORD mighty in battle."

Ps. 31:2   "Turn your ear to me, come quickly to my rescue; be my rock of refuge, a <u>strong</u> fortress to save me."

Ps. 61:3   "For you have been my refuge, a <u>strong</u> tower against the foe."

Ps. 62:11   "One thing God has spoken, two things I have heard, that you, O God, are <u>strong</u>, and that you, O Lord, are loving."

Ps. 89:10   "You crushed Rahab like one of the slain; with your <u>strong</u> arm you scattered your enemies."

Ps. 89:13   "Your arm is endowed with power; your hand is <u>strong</u>, your right hand exalted."

Ps. 140:7   "Sovereign Lord, my <u>strong</u> deliverer, who shields my head in the day of battle."

a. Hebrew/Strong's/biblical use

- mighty, strong
- strength and might
- strength and security

b. Other versions/translations

- house of defense
- mighty
- powerful
- stronghold, strength

c. Praise & Prayer Journal

1. What is strong about the Lord? (Answers include: He is mighty, a strong fortress, a tower, a strong hand and mighty arm, a deliverer.)

2. When did God exhibit His strong nature? (Answers include: against Pharaoh, for Moses and Joshua in their battles, against the army of and walls of Jericho.)

3. What are other biblical examples of this characteristic, attribute, or action of God? (Answers include: seating David on the throne, His ultimate restoration of Job, Elijah's faith in God in the contest with the prophets and gods of Baal, God's strength throughout the book of Revelation.)

4. When has God been strong for you and your family?

95 STRONGHOLD: God is our refuge, fortress, and defense. He provides safety, a defense, and rescues us.

Ps. 9:9	"The LORD is a refuge for the oppressed, a <u>stronghold</u> in times of trouble."
Ps. 18:2	". . . my <u>stronghold</u>."
Ps. 27:1	"The LORD is the <u>stronghold</u> of my life."
Ps. 31:2	". . . a <u>strong</u> fortress to save me."
Ps. 34:7	"The angel of the LORD <u>encamps around</u> those who fear him."
Ps. 37:39	"He is their <u>stronghold</u> in time of trouble."
Ps. 43:2	"You are God my <u>stronghold</u>."
Ps. 48:8	"God makes her secure forever."
Ps. 52:7	"'Here now is the man who did not make God his <u>stronghold</u> but trusted in his great wealth and grew strong by destroying others!'"
Ps. 144:2	"He is my loving God and my fortress, my <u>stronghold</u> and my deliverer, my shield, in whom I take refuge, who subdues peoples under me."

a. Hebrew/Strong's/biblical use

• deliverance, salvation, rescue, safety, welfare
• a fastness, castle, defense, fortress, stronghold, strong place

- place or means of safety, protection, refuge, stronghold
- a refuge, defense, high fort (tower)

b. Other versions/translations

- defense
- fortress; fort
- granite hideout
- high tower; house of defense
- life's fortress

- provides safety; place of safety; protector
- refuge
- sanctuary; strength; safe haven; shelters

c. Praise & Prayer Journal

1. When is God a stronghold for us? (Answers include: in times of trouble, of my life, to save me, to secure forever, as my place of stronghold.)

2. When has God shown His mighty strongholds?

3. What are biblical examples of this characteristic, attribute, or action of God? (Answers include: David while hiding among the caves and literal strongholds in the desert; for Joshua; in Nahum, the LORD is a stronghold in the day of trouble; in Joel, the LORD is a stronghold to the sons of Israel.)

4. What have been examples of God providing a stronghold for you and your family?

96 SUPPORTS: God protects, helps, holds up, comforts, strengthens, and He is my defense and reinforcement.

Ps. 18:18   " . . . but the LORD was my support."

Ps. 20:2   " . . . and grant you support from Zion."

Ps. 94:18   "When I said, 'My foot is slipping,' your unfailing love, LORD, supported me."

a. Hebrew/Strong's/biblical use

- help, aid
- refresh self, strengthen
- a support, a protector, sustenance
- to be upheld
- to comfort, establish, hold up

b. Other versions/translations

- came to my defense
- continued to hold up
- helped me; help; hold me up
- kept from falling
- reinforcements
- stay; supported; stuck by me
- took hold and held me fast

c. Praise & Prayer Journal

1. Where does true support come from? (Answers include: the LORD, from Zion.)

2. In the Bible, who did God support? (Answers include: Moses dealing with Pharaoh; His people, the Israelites, in the desert with food and protection for forty years; Moses and Joshua in their battles; Joseph, Mary, and Jesus with gifts from the three wise men, and as they fled to Egypt after Christ's birth.)

3. What are other biblical examples of this characteristic, attribute, or action of God? (Other Scriptures include: God is with us wherever we go [Joshua 1:9]; God supports us in many ways [2 Samuel 22:3, 4]; The LORD is "on my side" [Psalm 118:6]; God will strengthen and help us [Isaiah 41:10]; "The LORD your God is in your midst" [Zephaniah 3:17].)

4. When has God supported you and your family or kept you from falling?

97

SUSTAINS: God allows us to lean upon and rest upon; He comforts, holds up, refreshes, helps, continues to support, carries our load, keeps me going, lifts up, protects, relieves, takes care of me, watches over me, and we can lean and rest upon Him.

Ps. 3:5   "I wake again, because the LORD <u>sustains</u> me."

Ps. 18:35   " . . . and your right hand <u>sustains</u> me."

Ps. 41:3   "The LORD <u>sustains</u> them on their sickbed and restores them from their bed of illness. "

Ps. 54:4   "Surely God is my help; the LORD is the one who <u>sustains</u> me."

Ps. 55:22   "Cast your cares on the LORD and he will <u>sustain</u> you."

Ps. 119:116   "<u>Sustain</u> me, my God, according to your promise, and I will live; do not let my hopes be dashed."

Ps. 119:175   "Let me live that I may praise you and may your laws <u>sustain</u> me."

Ps. 146:9   "The LORD watches over the foreigner and <u>sustains</u> the fatherless and the widow, but he frustrates the ways of the wicked."

Ps. 147:6   "The LORD <u>sustains</u> the humble but casts the wicked to the ground."

a. Hebrew/Strong's/biblical use

- to help, support
- to lean, lay, rest, support, put, uphold, lean upon
- to support, comfort, establish, hold up, refresh self, strengthen, be upholding

b. Other versions/translations

- continues to support; carries our load
- gives strength
- held me up; help me
- keeps me going; keeps me alive
- lifts up
- protects; provider for my life

- relieves
- supported; strengthen
- takes care of
- takes good care of

- takes my side
- takes the side of
- upholds
- watching over me

c. Praise & Prayer Journal

1. Whom does God, the LORD, sustain? (Answers include: me [five times from the Psalms list above], the humble, fatherless, widow, those on their sick bed.)

2. How do we obtain God's sustaining? (Answers include: by casting our cares on the LORD, by His promise, by His law.)

3. What are biblical examples of this characteristic, attribute, or action of God? (Scriptures include: "The spirit of God has made me and the breadth of the Almighty gives me life" [Job 33:4]; "For the LORD God is my strength and my song" [Isaiah 12:2]; "He gives power to the faint and to him who has no might he increases strength" [Isaiah 40:29]; The LORD is good, "a stronghold in the day of trouble" [Nahum 1:7]. Other Scriptures include: Isaiah 26:3, 41:10; Jeremiah 10:12; Lamentations 3:22, 23; Zechariah 4:6.)

4. When has God sustained you and your family? When have you leaned and rested on Him?

98	**TEACHES**: God instructs, imparts knowledge, leads, points out, trains me, and allows me to learn God's pathway, laws, will, and decrees.

Ps. 25:4	"Show me your ways, O LORD, <u>teach</u> me your paths."
Ps. 25:5	" . . . guide me in your truth and <u>teach</u> me."
Ps. 25:9	" . . . and <u>teaches</u> them his way."
Ps. 27:11	"<u>Teach</u> me your way, O LORD . . . "

Ps. 32:8	"I will instruct you and <u>teach</u> you in the way you should go; I will counsel you with my loving eye on you."
Ps. 86:11	"<u>Teach</u> me your way, Lᴏʀᴅ, that I may rely on your faithfulness; give me an undivided heart, that I may fear your name."
Ps. 90:12	"<u>Teach</u> us to number our days, that we may gain a heart of wisdom."
Ps. 94:10	"Does he who disciplines nations not punish? Does he who <u>teaches</u> mankind lack knowledge?"
Ps. 94:12	"Blessed is the one you discipline, Lᴏʀᴅ, the one you <u>teach</u> from your law."
Ps. 119:12	"Praise be to you, Lᴏʀᴅ; <u>teach</u> me your decrees."
Ps. 119:26	"I gave an account of my ways and you answered me; <u>teach</u> me your decrees."
Ps. 119:29	"Keep me from deceitful ways; be gracious to me and <u>teach</u> me your law."
Ps. 119:33	"<u>Teach</u> me, Lᴏʀᴅ, the way of your decrees, that I may follow it to the end."
Ps. 119:64	"The earth is filled with your love, Lᴏʀᴅ; <u>teach</u> me your decrees."
Ps. 119:66	"<u>Teach</u> me knowledge and good judgment, for I trust your commands."
Ps. 119:68	"You are good, and what you do is good; <u>teach</u> me your decrees."
Ps. 119:108	"Accept, Lᴏʀᴅ, the willing praise of my mouth and <u>teach</u> me your laws."
Ps. 119:124	"Deal with your servant according to your love and <u>teach</u> me your decrees."
Ps. 119:135	"Make your face shine on your servant and <u>teach</u> me your decrees."
Ps. 119:171	"May my lips overflow with praise, for you <u>teach</u> me your decrees."
Ps. 132:12	"If your sons keep my covenant and the statutes I <u>teach</u> them, then their sons will sit on your throne forever and ever."
Ps. 143:10	"<u>Teach</u> me to do your will, for you are my God; may your good Spirit lead me on level ground."

a. Hebrew/Strong's/biblical use

- to instruct, teach
- to learn, teach

b. Other versions/translations

- grant me
- instruct; imparts knowledge
- lead me

- point out; point me
- school me
- taught, train me

c. Praise & Prayer Journal

1. What do the psalmists ask God to teach us? (Answers include: His paths, His ways [four times in the Psalms list], the way to go, to number our days, His law [two times from the Psalms list], His decrees [eight times from the Psalms list], to do His will.)

2. What are biblical examples of this characteristic, attribute, or action of God? (Scriptures include: to teach you what you are to say [Exodus 4:12]; "I will teach you what you are to do" [Exodus 4:15]; "teach them the good way in which they should walk" [1 Kings 8:36]; "teach me what I do not see" [Job 34:22]; "to whom would he teach knowledge" [Isaiah 28:9]; "for his God instructs and teaches him properly" [Isaiah 28:26]; "all your sons will be taught of the Lord" [Isaiah 54:13]; "they have turned their back to me and not their face, though I taught them, teaching again and again" [Jeremiah 32:33]; "that he may teach us about his ways and that we may walk in his paths" [Micah 4:2]; "and they shall all be taught of God" [John 6:45].)

3. When has God taught you and your family? In ways like learning His ways, paths, laws, His will, and His decrees?

99 TRUST/TRUSTWORTHY: God imparts truth and faithfulness; He supports, confirms, and always does what He says; He is dependable, reliable, and faithful, and we can place our confidence in Him.

Ps. 13:5   "But I <u>trust</u> in your unfailing love; my heart rejoices in your salvation."

Ps. 19:7   "The law of the LORD is perfect, refreshing the soul. The statutes of the LORD are <u>trustworthy</u>, making wise the simple."

Ps. 20:7   "Some <u>trust</u> in chariots and some in horses, but we <u>trust</u> in the name of the Lord our God."

Ps. 22:4   "In you our ancestors put their <u>trust</u>; they <u>trusted</u> and you delivered them."

Ps. 25:2   "I <u>trust</u> in you; do not let me be put to shame, nor let my enemies triumph over me."

Ps. 26:1   "I have <u>trusted</u> in the Lord without wavering."

Ps. 31:6   "I hate those who cling to worthless idols; as for me, I <u>trust</u> in the Lord."

Ps. 31:14   "But I <u>trust</u> in you, Lord; I say, 'You are my God.'"

Ps. 33:21   "In him our hearts rejoice, for we <u>trust</u> in his holy name."

Ps. 37:3   "<u>Trust</u> in the Lord and do good; dwell in the land and enjoy safe pasture."

Ps. 37:5   "Commit your way to the Lord; <u>trust</u> in him and he will do this."

Ps. 40:4   "Blessed is the man who makes the Lord his <u>trust</u>."

Ps. 52:8   "I <u>trust</u> in God's unfailing love for ever and ever."

Ps. 56:3   "When I am afraid, I put my <u>trust</u> in you."

Ps. 56:4   "In God, whose word I praise, in God I <u>trust</u>; I will not be afraid."

Ps. 56:11   "In God I <u>trust</u>; I will not be afraid."

Ps. 62:8   "<u>Trust</u> in him at all times, you people pour out your hearts to him, for God is our refuge."

Ps. 78:7   " . . . then they would put their <u>trust</u> in God."

Ps. 86:4   "Bring joy to your servant, Lord, for I put my <u>trust</u> in you."

Ps. 91:2   "I will say of the Lord, 'He is my refuge and my fortress, my God, in whom I <u>trust</u>.'"

Ps. 111:7   "The works of his hands are faithful and just; all his precepts are <u>trustworthy</u>."

Ps. 115:9   "<u>Trust</u> in the Lord—he is their help and shield."

Ps. 115:11 "You who fear him, <u>trust</u> in the Lord—he is their help and shield."

Ps. 119:66 "Teach me knowledge and good judgment, for I <u>trust</u> your commands."

Ps. 119:86 "All your commands are <u>trustworthy</u>; help me, for I am being persecuted without cause."

Ps. 119:138   "The statues you have laid down are righteous; they are fully <u>trustworthy</u>."

Ps. 125:1   "Those who <u>trust</u> in the LORD are like Mount Zion, which cannot be shaken but endures forever."

Ps. 145:13   "The LORD is <u>trustworthy</u> in all he promises and faithful in all he does."

a. Hebrew/Strong's/biblical use

- firmness, fidelity, steadfastness, steadiness
- to believe, support, confirm, be faithful
- to trust
- truth, firmness, faithfulness

b. Other versions/translations

- always does what He says
- believed
- boast
- clear
- confidence
- dependable
- faithful
- guaranteed
- hope
- looking to you
- places confidence in
- rely, reliable
- remember
- sure, sure thing
- throw myself on you
- trusted, trustworthy

c. Praise & Prayer Journal

1. Who or what should we trust in? (Answers include: the name of the LORD our God, in the LORD, in Him at all times, His unfailing love, His holy name, His commands.)

2. What is trustworthy? (Answers include: His statutes, precepts, commands, promises.)

3. What are biblical examples of this characteristic, attribute, or action of God? (Answers include: Noah trusting God with His plans to build a multilevel, massive, barge-type boat, the ark, with a zoo-like collection of animals; Moses trusting God in dealing with Pharaoh; Joshua conquering enemies in the Promised Land; Rahab [Joshua 2:1-24]; David [Psalm 23:1, 2]; other Scriptures include: Isaiah 43:2, 3; Proverbs 3:5, 6.)

4. When have you trusted God, and when has He proven trustworthy?

100

UPHOLDS: God accomplishes, supports, helps, maintains, comforts, defends, and He will give justice.

Ps. 9:4	"For you have <u>upheld</u> my right and my cause, sitting enthroned as the righteous judge."
Ps. 37:17	" . . . but the LORD <u>upholds</u> the righteous."
Ps. 37:24	" . . . for the LORD <u>upholds</u> him with his hand."
Ps. 63:8	"I cling to you; your right hand <u>upholds</u> me."
Ps. 82:3	"Defend the weak and the fatherless; <u>uphold</u> the cause of the poor and the oppressed."
Ps. 119:117	"<u>Uphold</u> me, and I will be delivered; I will always have regard for your decrees."
Ps. 140:12	"I know that the LORD secures justice for the poor and <u>upholds</u> the cause of the needy."
Ps. 145:14	"The LORD <u>upholds</u> all who fall and lifts up all who are bowed down."
Ps. 146:7	"He <u>upholds</u> the cause of the oppressed and gives food to the hungry."

a. Hebrew/Strong's/biblical use

- be just, be righteous
- to do, make, accomplish, fashion
- to help, follow close, maintain, retain, stay up
- to lean, lay, rest, support, uphold, lean upon
- to support, comfort, established, hold up, refresh self, strengthen

b. Other versions/translations

- continues to support
- defends my cause; does justice
- executes justice
- holds; holds me securely, helps
- judged in my favor
- maintained

- protect
- sustains, supports, sticks with
- took over, takes care of

- vindicates
- will give justice

c. Praise & Prayer Journal

1. Who or what does God uphold? (Answers include: the righteous, the cause of the poor, the oppressed, the needy, those who fail, providing food to the hungry and those who are bowed down.)

2. What are biblical examples of this characteristic, attribute, or action of God? (Examples and Scriptures include: Moses dealing with Pharaoh; God providing manna in the desert for forty years; "The Lord's right hand and strong arm for us" [Psalm 139:10, 16:11, 48:10, 73:23, 60:5, 108:6, 17:7, 98:1, 138:7, 18:35, 21:8, 45:4, 118:15, 16, 110:1]; Jesus sits at the right hand of God [Psalm 110:1, Matthew 22:44, Mark 12:36, Luke 20:42, 22:69, Acts 2:34, Acts 7:55, 56, 1 Peter 3:27, Revelation 5:1-7.)

3. When has God supported, comforted, maintained, or defended you or your family?

 WARRIOR: God can fight, do battle with might and strength, and He can save us.

Ps. 78:65   "Then the Lord awoke as from sleep, as a <u>warrior</u> wakes..."

a. Hebrew/Strong's/biblical use

- might, strong
- to fight, to do battle

- to save
- to send, send away

b. Other versions/translations

- mighty man

- strong man

c. Praise & Prayer Journal

1. When has God exhibited warrior characteristics? (Answers include: keeping Pharaoh's army from reaching His people as they were leaving Egypt, the walls of Jericho falling, helping David kill Goliath, helping David in his many battles and in his escapes.)

2. What are other biblical examples of this characteristic, attribute, or action of God? (Scriptures include: The Lord is a man of war [Exodus 15:3]; "The Lord, strong and mighty, the Lord, mighty in battle" [Psalm 24:8]; "The Lord goes out like a mighty man, like a man of war" [Isaiah 42:12]; Jeremiah, who said the Lord was "with him as a warrior" [Jeremiah 20:11]; put on the whole armor of God, with might and strength [Ephesians 6:10-18].)

3. When has God been a warrior for you or your family in fighting your battles?

102

WATCHES: God actively looks down; He sees all mankind and He sees everyone; He keeps his eyes on those who fear him and on the righteous both now and forevermore.

Ps. 1:6   "For the LORD <u>watches</u> over the way of the righteous."

Ps. 11:4   "The LORD is in his holy temple; the LORD is on his heavenly throne. He <u>observes</u> everyone on earth; his eyes examine them."

Ps. 33:13   "From heaven the LORD <u>looks</u> down and sees all mankind."

Ps. 33:14   " . . . from his dwelling place he <u>watches</u> all who live on earth."

Ps. 33:18   "But the <u>eyes</u> of the LORD are on those who fear him."

Ps. 34:15   "The <u>eyes</u> of the LORD are on the righteous."

Ps. 35:22   "O LORD, you have <u>seen</u> this; be not silent."

Ps. 39:13   "<u>Look</u> away from me, that I may rejoice again before I depart and am no more."

Ps. 66:7   "He rules forever by his power, his eyes <u>watch</u> the nations—let not the rebellious rise up against him."

Ps. 80:14	"Return to us, God Almighty! Look down from heaven and see! <u>Watch</u> over this vine."
Ps. 121:3	"He will not let your foot slip—he who <u>watches</u> over you will not slumber."
Ps. 121:4	"Indeed, he who <u>watches</u> over Israel will neither slumber nor sleep."
Ps. 121:5	"The LORD <u>watches</u> over you."
Ps. 121:7	"The LORD will keep you from all harm—he will <u>watch</u> over your life."
Ps. 121:8	"The LORD will <u>watch</u> over your coming and going both now and forevermore."
Ps. 127:1	"Unless the LORD builds the house, the builders labor in vain. Unless the LORD <u>watches</u> over the city, the guards stand <u>watch</u> in vain."
Ps. 141:3	"Set a guard over my mouth, LORD; keep <u>watch</u> over the door of my lips."
Ps. 142:3	"When my spirit grows faint within me, it is you who <u>watch</u> over my way."
Ps. 145:20	"The LORD <u>watches</u> over all who love him, but all the wicked he will destroy."

a. Hebrew/Strong's/biblical use

- glance sharply at
- to keep, guard, observe
- to know
- to look at
- to look out or about, spy, keep watch, observe, watch
- to see
- watchfulness

b. Other versions/translations

- behold
- charts; come to help
- guards, gaze; guardian
- have regard for
- knoweth; knows; keepeth; keeps; keeper
- looks
- observes; overlooks
- protector; preserve; protect
- sees; sticks by
- takes notice; take care of
- visit

c. Praise & Prayer Journal

1. Who are the eyes of the LORD kept on? (Answers include: those who fear Him, the righteous.)

2. Who does the LORD watch over? (Answers include: all who love Him, the way of the righteous, Israel, you, your life, the city, "the door of my lips," my way, all who live on earth.)

3. How does God watch? (Among the answers: He actively looks down, He sees all mankind and everyone, He keeps his eyes on those who fear Him, and on the righteous both now and forevermore.)

4. What are biblical examples of this characteristic, attribute, or action of God? (Among the answers: Abraham, Isaac, Jacob, Joseph, Job, Daniel; Daniel's friends Shadrach, Meshach, and Abednego; the great prophets like Isaiah, Jeremiah, and Nehemiah.)

5. When have you been thankful that God watched over you and your family?

103 WONDERFUL: God is marvelous, miraculous, and amazingly awesome.

Ps. 9:1	"I will give thanks to you, LORD, with all my heart; I will tell of all your <u>wonderful</u> deeds."
Ps. 26:7	" . . . proclaiming aloud your praise and telling of all your <u>wonderful</u> deeds."
Ps. 31:21	"Praise be to the LORD, for he showed his <u>wonderful</u> love to me."
Ps. 75:1	"We praise you, God, we praise you, for your Name is near; people tell of your <u>wonderful</u> deeds."
Ps. 107:8	"Let them give thanks to the LORD for his unfailing love and his <u>wonderful</u> deeds for mankind."
Ps. 107:24	"They saw the works of the LORD, his <u>wonderful</u> deeds in the deep."
Ps. 119:18	"Open my eyes that I may see <u>wonderful</u> things in your law."
Ps. 119:27	"Cause me to understand the way of your precepts that I may meditate on your <u>wonderful</u> deeds."

Ps. 119:129   "Your statutes are <u>wonderful</u>; therefore I obey them."

Ps. 139:14   "I praise you because I am fearfully and <u>wonderfully</u> made; your works are <u>wonderful</u>, I know that full well."

Ps. 145:5   "They speak of the glorious splendor of your majesty—and I will meditate on your <u>wonderful</u> works."

a. Hebrew/Strong's/biblical use

- a miracle, marvelous thing, wonder, wonderful, wonderfully
- a sign
- to be marvelous, wonderful

b. Other versions/translations

- amazing
- awesome
- marvelous miracles
- miracle: wonders
- wondrous

c. Praise & Prayer Journal

1. What is wonderful about God? (Answers include: His deeds [used six times in the Psalms list above], His statutes, things in His law, His works; what a wonderful God we have: He is the Father of our LORD Jesus Christ, the source of every mercy, the One who so wonderfully comforts and strengthens us in our hardships and trials.)

2. What are biblical examples of this characteristic, attribute, or action of God? (Answers include: all creation, seen and unseen; making Adam from the dust, and making Eve from Adam's rib; the parting of the Red Sea; other Scriptures include: God's deeds, statutes, works, and law are great, and He causes His wonderful works to be remembered [Psalm 111:24]; He is the God of all comfort [2 Corinthians 1:3].)

3. When has God been wonderful to you and your family?

104

WONDERS: God does marvelous works and deeds, miracles, miraculous signs, and amazing things.

Ps. 17:7   "Show me the <u>wonders</u> of your great love, you who save by your right hand those who take refuge in you from their foes."

Ps. 31:21   "Praise be to the Lord, for he showed me the <u>wonders</u> of his love when I was in a city under siege."

Ps. 40:5   "Many, Lord my God, are the <u>wonders</u> you have done, the things you planned for us."

Ps. 65:8   "The whole earth is filled with awe at your <u>wonders</u>."

Ps. 78:11   "They forgot what he had done, the <u>wonders</u> he had shown them."

Ps. 88:10   "Do you show your <u>wonders</u> to the dead?"

Ps. 89:5   "The heavens praise your <u>wonders</u>, O Lord."

Ps. 105:5   "Remember the <u>wonders</u> he has done."

Ps. 111:4   "He has caused his <u>wonders</u> to be remembered; the Lord is gracious and compassionate."

Ps. 135:9   "He sent his signs and <u>wonders</u> into your midst, Egypt, against Pharaoh and all his servants."

Ps. 136:4   " . . . to him who alone does great <u>wonders</u>."

a. Hebrew/Strong's/biblical use

- a miracle—marvelous thing
- sign, miracle, portent
- to be marvelous, be wonderful
- wonderful, wonderfully

b. Other versions/translations

- amazing things, amazing deeds
- awesome deeds
- marvelous deeds
- marvelous, miraculous things, miraculous signs
- marvels, marvelous works
- mighty miracles
- wondrously, wonderful works

c. Praise & Prayer Journal

1. What wonders of God are mentioned in the Bible? (Answers include: His great love, His love when under attack, what He has made, the whole earth.)

2. What are some of the wonders God has done? (Answers include: the miracles in Egypt against Pharaoh, the parting of the Red Sea, Balaam's donkey speaking, rescuing Daniel through interpretation of dreams and in the lion's den, rescuing Daniel's friends in the fire.)

3. What are other biblical examples of this characteristic, attribute, or action of God? (Scriptures include: Job recounts that God's hand is the life of every creature and the breath of all mankind [Job 12:7-10]; consider God's wonders: clouds, lightning, earth, mountains, seas, land [Job 37:14-16]; other Scriptures include: Psalm 19:1; Psalm 95:4, 5; Psalm 104:24, 25; Isaiah 24:4-6; Isaiah 43:20; Ezekiel 34:2, 3; Romans 1:20; John 1:3.)

4. What wonders of God have you seen displayed in your life and your family's life?

Notes

Notes

Notes

Notes

Notes

Notes

Notes

Notes